From Democracy to Nazism

Rudolf Heberle

From
DEMOCRACY
To
NAZISM

A Regional Case Study on Political Parties in Germany

New York · HOWARD FERTIG · 1970

Preface to the 1970 Edition

Nearly twenty-five years have passed since the first publication of this book, and a third of a century has gone by since the completion of the research on which it is based.

How I came to write it is told in the preface to the 1945 edition. At that time the interest in its subject, which had been lively during the war, had subsided as a result of the preoccupation with the pressing problems of the postwar period. When, about ten years later, professional circles again showed interest in the content as well as the method of this study and demands for copies increased, it was discovered that a large part of the stock had been destroyed. Soon the book was out of print. To find oneself the producer of a rare book is not exactly gratifying. I therefore welcomed the opportunity offered by Howard Fertig to have this little book reprinted.

From Democracy to Nazism gained attention for two reasons: it was the first thorough empirical study of the Nazi movement, and the methods used aroused interest among social scientists engaged in the study of elections and political behavior in general. Scandinavian scholars, foremost among them Sten S. Nilson, were among the first to take notice. In America, S. M. Lipset in *Political Man* and other publications has repeatedly referred to my findings. In Germany, a historian, G. Stoltenberg, presently minister in the Federal Government, published in *1962* a book entitled *Politische Strömungen in Schleswig-holsteinischen Landvolk 1918–1933* which is based on my work (I had given him access to the German manuscript) and on other sources which had become available. His work is a complement to mine. Finally, the Institut für Zeitgeschichte in Munich, on the advice of a group of eminent historians and political scientists, decided to publish the entire manuscript as it had been completed in 1934, as a document of contemporary history. This was published in 1963 under the title *Landbevölkerung und Nationalsozialismus. Eine soziologische Untersuchung der politischen Willensbildung in Schleswig-Holstein 1918–1932.*

From the methodological point of view, *From Democracy to Nazism* aroused the interest of a number of younger scholars, particularly in France, who, like myself, were following in the footsteps of André Siegfried in developing the ecological method of analyzing political elections. In the United States this method had for some time been neglected in favor of social-psychological studies of voting behavior, using survey data. Recently, a combination of the two approaches is coming into use. The two methods complement each other in several ways: past elections which occurred before the development of polls and surveys can be analyzed only by the ecological method, and the choice of samples for surveys can be facilitated by the use of ecological data. Needless to say, under the political conditions prevailing in Germany at the time of my research, the ecological method was the only one applicable. I was, however, fortunate in that I had the opportunity of interviewing a number of people who were or had been prominent in public life. Many of these interviews were conducted after the seizure of power by the Nazis and could not therefore, as a rule, probe directly into political opinions.

But the research project involved more than political ecology. It required a combination of sociological observations, analysis of economic conditions of political significance, and historical perspective. The last was important because the Nazi movement was not simply Hitler's creation but developed from various antecedents.

The general scheme for the analysis, or model as one would say today, was borrowed from André Siegfried's classic work. It had, however, to be modified because the problem of my study was different. Siegfried wanted to explain the constancy of the political climate of his region, that is, the continuity of basic political attitudes in a society where the party system was extremely fluid. My problem, on the other hand, was to find the factors which had led to a radical change in the political climate of the region in a society where the older political parties were well organized and had survived the First World War and the revolution of 1918.

It may be appropriate to state the differences between my two books more precisely than was done in the preface to the 1945 edition. The main body of *From Democracy to Nazism* gives the quintessence of the much more elaborate German work; the introductory and the concluding chapters of *From Democracy to Nazism* are not contained in *Landbevölkerung und Nationalsozialismus*, however. They were written while the Second World War was still going on and must be read in this context. One could not at that time foresee the partition of Germany under two diametrically opposed regimes. But so far as West Germany, the Bundesrepublik Deutschland, is concerned, the postwar political development has been essentially as I anticipated, at least to this date.

Finally, the reader will easily realize that much can be gained from this study in attempting to understand certain recent political tendencies and movements (somewhat vaguely called the "extreme right") in the United States today.

Baton Rouge, La.
January 1969

Rudolf Heberle

PREFACE

THE following collection of papers consists of studies which I have pursued at different times. The first paper, and to some extent the last, is an attempt to answer certain questions which I have been asked to discuss in lectures on various occasions since my immigration to the United States. The first and last papers deal with National Socialism in general and are published here for the first time.

The second, third, and fourth papers have been salvaged from a comprehensive regional study which I began twelve years ago. At that time the impending political crisis in Germany incited one to observe and analyze the political forces that threatened or sustained the democratic regime. The University of Kiel, located in a region which during those years was the scene of many turbulent conflicts between the antagonistic forces, offered an excellent observation post for the kind of intensive regionally limited study of political parties and movements which I felt was needed and for which I hoped to set an example. A generous grant-in-aid from the Rockefeller Foundation enabled me to carry out my plan during the years 1932 to 1934.

Political conditions made publication of the book impossible. Only in recent years have I been able to publish at least the main results, in the form of two papers in the *Journal of Politics* (1943) and the *American Sociological Review* (1944), which are reproduced, with some additions and alterations, as chapters three and four in this volume. In the original manuscript the sequence of these chapters was reversed; the ecological study formed the main parts and the historical treatment was presented at the end. The present arrangement will, I believe, be better adapted to the American public, although it necessitates some repetitions in the text.

The second chapter is a condensed version of the introductory chapter of the original manuscript; it has not been published elsewhere.

It is hoped that these papers will not only help to throw light on the "causes" of Germany's tragic political course, but also aid in understanding and appraising the political forces in Germany on which we may be able to rely for the establishment of a lasting peace.

Today, as we see more clearly the true nature of National Socialism than we did at the time when the regional studies were made, it seems even more strange and incredible that such large masses of generally sober-minded and freedom-loving North Germans, who were not at all accustomed to a tradition of authoritarian government, should have trusted a man like Hitler and his party with the political future of their country.

The following discussions should contribute an answer to the questions of whether and to what extent the Nazi regime can be considered an outgrowth of permanent dispositions and characteristics of the German people and to what extent it has to be understood as an anomalous phenomenon, which, after Hitler's defeat, may be overcome by forces more in harmony with Western political tradition.

A few methodological remarks may be justified. These studies do not aim at an analysis of German political ideas in general, nor do they attempt to uncover the sources of National Socialist ideology in past political thought. They are rather concerned, primarily, with those organized groups and unorganized social collectivities in which political ideas become effective. In a nation with a long history of political and philosophical thought like the German, any political movement and party will in its ideology show more or less the imprint of all important and influential ideas that have appeared in the past.

It is fascinating to trace these spiritual influences; but more important for the sociological understanding of a political movement is a study of its immediate antecedents or forerunners among those political circles and movements in which political and politically relevant ideas are debated, modified, and propagated. It is the continuity of these groups of men and women of flesh and blood which constitutes the social basis for the continuity of ideas. This sociological continuity is of much greater practical importance than the mere spiritual continuity that also exists between ideas, taken in abstraction from their human creators and carriers.

It is also important to understand that a political movement or party cannot be characterized by a single idea but rather that it is the constellation of ideas characteristic of a given political movement which constitutes its ideological peculiarity and which is of practical significance in political life. The ideas which form such constellations are seldom logically consistent; they are often quite contradictory. Their coexistence in the same movement can be explained only if one detects the underlying interests of the various social groups of which the movement or party is composed.

It is impossible to name all those who, during various phases of my studies, gave their advice and assistance. I appreciate in particular the aid received through the Institute for Population Research at Louisiana State University, which enabled me to complete this volume.

R. H.

Louisiana State University

CONTENTS

I

ORIGIN AND NATURE OF THE NATIONAL SOCIALIST PARTY

A T the eve of the First World War we find the following alignment of social classes and political parties in
Germany: The small landed nobility and the large landowners of middle class origin in the north German plains
east of the Elbe-Saale line formed the backbone of the
Conservative party. The wealthy farmers all over Protestant north Germany were in the same camp, with certain
exceptions to be mentioned later. The entrepreneurs in the
heavy industries, the mining interests and other groups of
manufacturers, fearful of the rising power of labor and
willing to trade protective tariffs for agricultural products
against industrial tariffs, had seceded from the right wing
of Liberalism and were supporting the Conservative or
the *Freikonservative* party (*Reichspartei*). To this party
belonged also some of the very large landowners, particularly in Silesia. The rest of the "business" classes were still
Liberal, but nationalistic and imperialistic. The *Nationalliberale* party, once—before they made their peace with
Bismarck—the great movement for unification of the
Reich and constitutional reform, had become a party of
rich merchants, shipowners, bankers, and the well-to-do
among the professional classes. Its main stronghold was
in northwestern Germany, particularly in the cities.

The smaller businessmen in commerce and manufacturing, the handicraft masters and a large part of the "new

middle class" of white-collar workers, also a considerable part of the professions, particularly in southwestern Germany, adhered to the left wing of Liberalism, the Progressive party, which opposed the increasing appropriations for army and navy and demanded constitutional reforms and transition to parliamentary government. Finally, labor was democratic and socialistic, especially in the larger industrial centers.

Cutting across all classes, the Catholic Center party, with its strongholds in the Rhineland and in Bavaria, did not stand for any particular economic and political program and had become, as Max Weber pointed out, more and more a "patronage party." In the system of parties it had become the tongue on the balance since, just because of its social heterogeneity, it could enter coalitions with the Conservatives as well as with the Progressives.

While a "close relation to ideology," as Neumann calls it, was characteristic of all German parties,[1] there emerged in the years before the First World War also a very close alliance of parties with economic interest organizations. The Social Democratic party was affiliated with the *Freie Gewerkschaften,* i. e., the socialist trade unions, while on the other extreme the Conservative party became more and more the political instrument of the *Bund der Landwirte,* the organization of large landowners. This tendency towards control of parties by organized economic blocks was the more dangerous for the political future of the nation since under the "constitutional monarchy" the powers and functions of the parties were limited virtually to the representation of the taxpayers' interests; they were not, as in England or other states with parliamentary government, channels for the selection of responsible states-

[1] S. Neumann, "Political Parties,—Germany," *Encyclopedia of the Social Sciences.*

men; nor were they, at least not the parties of the left, confronted with the possibility that they, as parties, would have to take the responsibility for their policy.[2] And yet, despite the firm entrenchment of the landed aristocracy with its predominance in bureaucracy and army, there was in the years between Bismarck's resignation and the beginning of the First World War a definite trend towards democratization and parliamentary regime.[3] This was bound to be so in view of the growing importance of wage earners and employees and the growing dissatisfaction among the small bourgeoisie with the imperial regime. Also, there was, as in England, a growing sense of responsibility for the lot of the working class in all strata of the nation.

The collapse of the imperial regime and of the monarchies in the federated states in 1918 led quite naturally to a weakening of the Conservative forces and brought the Liberal and Socialist forces into power. The Social Democratic party experienced a considerable reinforcement from hitherto unorganized elements of the labor class, from the lower middle class and even from the small farmers' class. The secession of the Independent Socialists, and of the Communists on the other hand, had of course a weakening effect.

The great mass of the old middle class of small independent businessmen, small farmers, large blocks of the professions, and intellectuals formed the new *Deutsche Demokratische Partei,* the heir of prewar Progressivism

[2] Max Weber, *Parlament und Regierung im Neugeordneten Deutschland* (Munich and Leipzig, 1918).

[3] See S. Neumann, *Die Deutschen Parteien* (Berlin, 1932), p. 118, n. 4. For a good analysis of German political opinion from 1871 to 1933, see Sydney L. W. Mellen, "The German People and the Postwar World, a Study Based on Election Statistics, 1871–1933," *The American Political Science Review* (August, 1943).

and the main support of the new constitution. Those parts of the middle classes which were more conservative, more imperialistic, but which still adhered to the principles of liberalism formed the *Deutsche Volkspartei*—Stresemann's party—which was also supported by the large export industries and commercial and shipping interests, as well as by the banking interests. This new party represented a fusion of right-wing Progressivism and left-wing National Liberalism. On the extreme right, a new Conservative party was formed under the euphemistic name of *Deutschnationale Volkspartei*. It was not so much a people's party as a coalition of the agrarian and big business interests and a rally of the counter-revolutionary forces.

The Center party, now that the parliamentary system was established, increased its power as the pivot of all possible coalition governments.

Such was, roughly, the alignment of parties and classes during the first years after the war.

It was a multiple party system, without a tradition in parliamentary democratic government; it was mortgaged with the responsibility for the ratification of the peace treaty, and it was launched in a time of economic distress and exhaustion; it was furthermore encumbered with the device of proportional representation which opened the doors of the Reichstag and the state parliaments to all sorts of political sects; and it was to face the most formidable economic crisis which the Western World had ever experienced. The inflation, which came to a climax in December, 1923, when the mark had fallen to $\frac{1}{1,000,000,000,000}$ of its original exchange value, swept away what the war had left of middle class savings and investments. By 1925 the numerical relation of "property" to "labor" interests was something like 20 per cent against 80 per cent of the population.[4]

After four short years of recovery and prosperity came the world depression in agriculture in 1928, followed by the general depression in 1929. The entire period from 1920 to 1933 was characterized by the growth of combinations, trusts, cartels, holding companies in manufacturing, in commerce, and in banking. The old middle class of independent businessmen was deprived of its financial reserves, was weakened in its economic influence, and suffered severe shocks to its sense of security. The "new middle class" of white-collar workers was divided in its political attitudes. While a strong minority of the unions of salaried employees and officials was affiliated with the Social Democratic party, the majority adhered to the non-Socialist parties. For a while a large block of salaried employees formed the left wing of the *Deutschnationale Partei*.

In this process the Liberal parties were ground up, split into minor parties and even clear-cut economic interest groups of creditors who desired revaluation of their claims, of real estate owners, of small farmers, and other pressure groups.

The Conservatives who gained considerable power in the mid-twenties came finally, in 1928, so definitely under the control of the heavy industry interests that several secessions occurred, representing farmers as well as salaried employees, professional groups and others who, while being opposed to the democratic regime, did not like Mr. Hugenberg's course.

At the same time certain changes had occurred in the

[4] Th. Geiger, *"Die Soziale Schichtung des Deutschen Volkes," Soziologische Gegenwartsfragen*, 1. Heft (Stuttgart, 1932).

structure of all the middle class parties. With the increase in membership which they had experienced after the war, with the necessity for maintaining a more rational and permanent organization, they had been compelled to follow the example of the Social Democrats and create a party bureaucracy. Proportional representation gave increased power to the party bureaus. These factors and the enormous size of election districts removed the campaigning politicians from close contact with the constituents. This again furnished pressure groups with the opportunity of placing their representatives on the ballots. Furthermore, leadership and bureaucracy in all parties, with the exception of the Communists, was superannuated.[5] Young men, however gifted politically, had scarcely a chance to advance to any influential position.

In foreign relations, finally, none of the democratic statesmen had been able to score a real, spectacular, impressive success.

It should not be difficult to understand why, in such circumstances, a party led by fanatic patriots, which denounced radically all the existing political parties, which claimed to be independent of any particular economic interests, the only true champion of the real people and the *avantgarde* of the awakening nation, would exert immense attraction for the uprooted middle class elements, for politically untrained youths, for political adventurers, and for counter-revolutionaries in general. Its appeal was strengthened by the fact that, in spite of being one of the most rationally organized and strictly disciplined parties the nation had ever seen, it proclaimed the anti-bureaucratic principle of leadership and, in its exacting

[5] See, for instance, A. Mendelssohn-Bartholdy, "The Political Dilemma in Germany," *Foreign Affairs,* Vol. 8 (July, 1930), p. 620.

demands of active participation on the rank and file, set a
new style in political action.

The Nazi party, as it emerged between 1930 and 1933,
was really the conflux or fusion of those numerous "racial"
or *voelkische* movements which had sprung up, largely by
secession from the Conservative camp, under the leadership of such men as Count Reventlow, von Graefe, Wulle,
"Knüppel" Kunze, Ludendorff, and others. Between 1925
and 1932 most of these political sects came to join forces
with their largest competitor, the Hitler movement. These
movements were strongly influenced by and closely linked
with the much older Pan-German movement.[6]

[6] Konrad Heiden, *Geschichte des Nationalsozialismus* (Berlin, 1932),
Ch. I. The *"Alldeutsche Verband"* was primarily an upper middle class
organization, whose membership consisted largely of teachers in secondary
schools and universities, small businessmen, lawyers, officials and other professional people and a few army and navy officers. (Mildred S. Wertheimer,
*The Pan-German League, 1890–1914, Studies in History, Economics and
Public Law* [Columbia University], Vol. 112, pp. 65 ff.) Numerically it was
never very strong and its influence in pre-Nazi Germany has been grossly
overestimated; yet as a source of National-Socialist ideology it is of great
importance. Hitler has repeatedly acknowledged his indebtedness to the
Pan-Germanists. As early as 1924, during the trial in Munich after the
November *putsch*, Hitler stated, "I left Vienna as an absolute Antisemite,
as an arch-enemy of the entire Marxistic philosophy, as Pan-German in
my political conviction. . . ." (*Der Hitler-Prozess, Auszuege aus den
Verhandlungsberichten* [Muenchen, 1924], p. 18.) Several leading Pan-
Germanists were granted recognition as "forerunners" in official Nazi
publications.

No other organization had in its program and in the writings of its
leaders reached such close relation to the Nazi creed. While many single
ideas which the Nazis have adopted are found in a wide variety of schools
of thought and social movements, there is nowhere else such close ap-
proximation to the very constellation of ideas which is characteristic of
the Nazis. The president of the Alldeutsche Verband, Heinrich Class, a
lawyer, using the pseudonym Einhart, wrote a brief history of the German
people (including the Germans abroad) which between 1909 and 1912
appeared in four editions and can be regarded as representative of the
political opinion of the Pan-Germans. It was widely read among middle

It was the secret of Hitler's power that he, who had
more appeal to the masses than any of the other radical
nationalists (with the possible exception of Gregor Stras-

class youth and certainly exerted a not inconsiderable influence on the
war generation, which became the generation of Nazi leaders. While
drawing a line of distinction between the kind of "rough and disorderly
anti-Semitism" that grew out of economic motivations and the "serious,
well justified cultural and political anti-Semitism" that is based on the
race idea, Class nevertheless considers the Jews, with the exception of
"a few morally and intellectually high standing families that can and
want to become Germans" (p. 292), as the internal enemies of the German
State, along with the Polish, French, and Danish minorities, the "Ultra-
montanists" in the Catholic Center party, the radical Liberals and the
Social Democrats. The list of enemies is identical with that of the Nazis—
only the Freemasons are missing. Class also sympathizes with the declin-
ing petty bourgeoisie (*Kleinbuergertum*) and holds a bias against big
business, particularly the Jewish department stores, although on the other
hand he is definitely an imperialist. He deplores the fact that the overseas
emigrants are lost to the German nation, serving merely as "cultural
fertilizer" in America, etc. He advocates repatriation of the German population in the eastern provinces and in Austria. He also warns that the
government should prepare for the time when the boundaries of the
Fatherland will be too narrow for the increasing masses of population,
while deploring on the other hand the decline of fertility in the cities (pp.
314–315). He severely criticizes the regime of the Kaiser, and he expresses
the hope and the expectation that there will come "the mighty man who,
aware of the disease of our age and of its dangers, will direct and use
the healing forces and will overcome those of decay" (p. 413). To prepare
his work of salvation is the task of "all faithful and sincere among the
people." These have to educate the nation to the realization of its destiny
and of the dangers by which it is surrounded. They have to teach the people
that "all Germans on this earth belong together by language and blood
and that the more fortunate among the '*Volksgenossen*' should not be indifferent towards the lot of the less fortunate; that this solidarity . . .
could be the most powerful weapon of German statesmanship. . . ." (p.
414). This task is already being tackled in the "Voelkischen Vereinen,"
the strengthening of which is the serious duty of all those who love their
people and country (*ibid.*).

After 1918 the Alldeutsche Verband developed the basic tenets of the new
racial state theory (see *Grundzuege des Voelkischen Staatsgedankens,* ed.
by the Alldeutsche Verband [ca. 1923], and the critical analysis by W.
Jarno, "Zur Kritik der Völkischen Bewegung," *Preussische Jahrbuecher,*
[1925].)

ser), was shrewd enough to balance the rival organizations within his movement, that he controlled the SA and SS and that, while he succeeded in concealing from the masses the counter-revolutionary nature of his policy, he was able to make the financiers of the party believe in its essentially conservative intentions. At the same time, the Hitler party, because of the leadership principle, opened a political career to anybody, regardless of wealth, education, age, experience, or intelligence—being the least discriminatory party of all; the only qualification that mattered was the unerring devotion to the party and unquestionable loyalty to the leader.

When the terrible depression with its mass unemployment cast its shadow on the people's minds, when masses of young voters grew up who had never had a permanent job or any job at all, the Nazi party offered at least activity, an outlet from the doldrums, and also shelter, food, and uniforms, attractions which made it a bitter competitor of the Communists in certain proletarian areas of the metropolitan cities, such as that roving-ground of the legendary Horst Wessel, in the slums of Berlin.

In the country, young men and also women who in normal times would have gone into industrial or other urban occupations found themselves caught, without prospect, in the unexciting and embittering atmosphere of depressed villages and towns. Again the Nazi movement, with its SA and SS, its truck rides from meeting to meeting all over the countryside and occasionally to a mass meeting in the big city, offered an outlet for penned-up energies and emotions.

These youngsters and many of the somewhat older war-generation who also had never found a real foothold in civilian life after their return from the trenches, ships, and garrisons could not know from experience what the actual issues were in public matters. No wonder that many among them, and often the more energetic and politically conscious, developed their own political dream-world, joining and quitting one of the little political sects after the other, until they finally drifted or were drafted into the least unrealistic among them, which soon was to develop into a veritable political church.

It should be noted, however, that the early support of the Hitler party came, in all social classes, from those who for some reason or other had failed to make a success in their business or occupation, and who had lost their social status or were in danger of losing it. Those who managed to weather the storms of postwar depression, inflation, and world-depression were seldom found among the sympathizers or supporters of the Hitler movement.

The masses of the organized party members consisted therefore before 1933 largely of people who were outsiders in their own class, black sheep in their families, thwarted in their ambitions—to a very large proportion unbalanced, maladjusted, cramped personalities.

To some extent this analysis applies also to the leading men in the party. Here, however, we have to make some modifications.

The original inner circle around Adolf Hitler, from the early days of the party, did not consist of lower middle class people (petty bourgeoisie, *Kleinbuerger*) but rather of sons of once-well-to-do businessmen and former high-ranking officials in the civil service. Most of these men had been officers in the war or had wanted to become professional officers; many had suffered considerable financial losses because of the war or the defeat. Most of them were ardent patriots, burning with desire for revenge, obsessed with hatred for those democratic statesmen who had signed the peace of Versailles and for the parties which they represented. They were, in an economic sense and to some extent in a social sense, "classless" political adventurers, conspirators, and fanatics. Their hatred of the existing classes was unevenly divided between the big business interests, who seemed only too anxious to resume normal relations with the enemy of yesterday, and the "Marxists," whom they accused of having caused the breakdown of the home front and of thereby having administered the "stab-in-the-back" to the allegedly undefeated forces at the front. Like most of their followers, these men had only a very limited experience in political life. As one critic of the new nationalism has very aptly remarked: their idea of the state and society was formed under conditions of war —adding that "one cannot see very far from a trench."

Having never held any office or leading position in one of the older parties, nor in a labor union or professional organization, having never seen democratic processes in action, they thought of politics in terms of conflict and combat rather than in terms of debate, compromise, and social integration. National Socialism meant to many of them simply: beat the Marxists first and then the French, the Poles, and all the rest.

However, not all of them were of this caliber: crackpot money reformers like Gottfried Feder, nationalistic Socialists like the Strassers, romantic dreamers and Russian emigrés like Rosenberg played a considerable part in shaping the ideology of the party and in winning votes and members.

The success of the party, the character of the regime which it later established and its responsibility for the Second World War are not understandable without consideration of another element in the original movement. In the turbulent days of 1918 to 1920, when the eastern provinces were threatened by Polish aggression, when the young democracy was endangered by local communistic regimes and by armed rebellions of radical and militant elements in the working class, the government had consented to the demand of the still incomplete *Reichswehr* to organize auxiliary forces of ex-soldiers and youthful volunteers. Some of these, gathered by leaders of magnetic personality, later formed the original cadres of the SA and SS. They set the tone and pattern for the political tactics. Some of the leaders were destined to become Gauleiters, chiefs of police, and other high dignitaries in the Third Reich.

It was because of the existence of this private army that Hitler enjoyed from the very beginning of his career the clandestine support of the *Reichswehr* command. The connections were so strong that the democratic Reichs government and the Prussian government found their hands tied every time they attempted to crush the Nazis by disbanding the SA and SS.[7]

In the early twenties these militant nationalists were the main force on which the *Reichswehr* commanders could rely in building up a secret reserve—the so-called *"schwarze Reichswehr."* Many of the SA and SS leaders of high rank were in fact ex-officers. Thus the NSDAP, by maintaining these organizations and keeping an officers' reserve in cold storage, lent a valuable service to the *Reichswehr*. The relations between the party and the army were therefore quite intimate from the very beginning and remained so in spite of certain tensions and minor conflicts. Incidentally, the Conservative private army, the Steel Helmets (*Stahlhelm*), attempted a similar function, with

---

[7] The relations between the Nazi movement and the *Reichswehr* are discussed in: Heiden, *op. cit.*, pp. 12 ff.; Herbert Rosinski, *The German Army*, Infantry Journal (Washington, D.C., 1944), pp. 114 ff.; Alfred Vagts, *Hitler's Second Army*, Infantry Journal (1943), pp. 14, 18–20, 96 ff.

somewhat less success, however, because it was top-heavy in the older age groups.

The navy was perhaps less in need of the pre-military resources of the party, although the Marine-SA probably had the sympathy of the admiralty. The new "Luftwaffe" was of course very largely an outgrowth of the Nazi party and its auxiliary and affiliated organizations.

It would be interesting but futile to speculate about the question of what would have happened to the German counter-revolution if the peacemakers of Versailles had failed to present it with the wonderful instrument of a professional army of 100,000 selected men and officers. But it is extremely important to understand properly the association between the army command and the National Socialists in order to avoid mistakes in the appraisal of the internal situation in Germany.[8]

On the other hand, the Hitler movement is not a continuation or outgrowth of the Prussian tradition. It is not even a fruit of conservatism. Herman Rauschning [9] and Helmut Kuhn [10] have made this very clear. The evidence is ample and manifold for the contention that the association of the army command with the Hitler organization, of

[8] The true significance of the events of July 20, 1944, cannot yet be ascertained. The most plausible interpretation is that the attempt at Hitler's life—whether it was genuine or staged—has been the pretext to eliminate all possible competitors in the inner circle of the Nazi party, leaving this group as the only real power in Germany with which peace negotiations might be opened. (See for instance the editorial "Die Notwendige Krise" in the usually well-informed London emigrant paper Die Zeitung, Aug. 25, 1944.)
Disagreements between army commanders and the political leadership seem to have been limited to questions of military strategy, but nothing indicates fundamental conflicts between army and party over ultimate political aims.

[9] H. Rauschning, The Revolution of Nihilism (New York, 1939).

[10] H. Kuhn, Freedom Forgotten and Remembered (Chapel Hill, N.C., 1943).

the Conservatives with the Nazis, was essentially a *ma-
riage de convenance*—a rational and temporary alliance
against common political adversaries. It is not our intention to acquit the army or the Conservatives of their responsibility for the tragedy which was brought over Germany by the Hitler regime, but it is of prime importance in
order to perceive clearly the dangerous nature of Nazism
that we should understand the profound contrasts between
National Socialism and Prussian conservatism.[11]

Before going into this discussion we may point out that
only a few among the leading Nazis were Prussians, that
the Hitler movement gained its first strongholds not in
Prussia but in Franconia, in Thuringia, and in other non-
Prussian regions and states, and that those Prussian provinces where the NSDAP in later years scored highest in
elections were—apart from the the eastern border provinces—the more recent acquisitions of Prussia.[12] We even

[11] The conservative position is described here at some length merely in
order to develop the antithesis of National Socialism to Western political
tradition. We are convinced that it would be a political mistake to engage
in any negotiations with conservative circles when the Hitler regime breaks
down. The Conservatives, by supporting Hitler, have forfeited any moral
claims to such recognition. Furthermore, they would not have a ghost
of a chance to win popular support in a postwar Germany; they could
rule only by assuming dictatorial powers. Failure to recognize that he
has been fighting for a lost cause is the main weakness in Rauschning's
otherwise very remarkable book.

The term "Prussian tradition" is of course quite vague, but so are the
ideas of "Prussianism" and the concept of "the *Junkers*" as they are used
in popular (and sometimes even in scholarly) discussion. "Conservatism"
also is one of those broad notions that would need more precise definition
to be applied in a sociological analysis. "Prussian Conservatism" comprises
several varieties of conservative thought and has gone through various
phases of development. (S. Neumann, *Die Stufen des Preussischen Kon-
servatismus, Historische Studien*, Heft 190 [Berlin, 1930].) In this discussion I had therefore to resort to considerable simplification.

[12] James K. Pollock, "An Areal Study of the German Electorate, 1930–
1933," *The American Political Science Review*, Vol. 28, No. 1 (February,
1944), pp. 89–103 (in particular p. 94).

believe that the anti-Prussian sentiment still powerful in these territories was one of the factors that contributed to the growth of Nazism. (See Chapter III.)

We can, however, support our thesis more directly by a brief confrontation of the main tenets of conservatism with those of National Socialism. The political creed of the old ruling class in Prussia who formed the core and mainstay of conservatism in Germany comprised three basic ideas: the state is founded on the principles of Christianity; [13] the government is bound by and subject to the law; and state-service, in the armed forces or other, is a noble duty inherent in citizenship.

It is true that conservative thinkers in Germany tended to endow the state with the character of a super-individual personality, the nature of which could not be explained in terms of a mere covenant of the citizens.[14] But this state, despite its super-rational dignity was not the ultimate ethical and political value: the individual, because of man's immediate relation to God,[15] is his own judge in ethical matters; if his conscience compels him to disagree with the sovereign, he has the right to express himself in words and actions. If he makes use of this right, even if this brings him into conflict with the positive law of the land, he is, by the same law, protected against arbitrary use of the state's power.[16] For the government itself is bound to obey the law—the civil law, the criminal law, the administrative law, and the constitutional law. The law consists

[13] A. von Martin, *Weltanschauliche Motive im Altkonservativen Denken;* in *Deutscher Staat und Deutsche Parteien* (Meinecke-Festschrift, 1922), pp. 361, 381.

[14] As a typical example of this doctrine, see Otto von Giercke, *Ueber das Wesen der menschlichen Verbaende* (Leipzig, 1902).

[15] See the discussion in Kuhn, *op. cit.*

[16] Even respect is due if his actions appear to be motivated by honest convictions. This is indicated by the provision for internment of political prisoners in certain cases, a penalty which is not dishonoring.

of general rules, properly enacted and modifiable only by a constitutionally prescribed procedure. It applies to all citizens, irrespective of rank or race, wealth or influence. In summary, the creed of conservatism was well in agreement with the essentials of Western civilization. The peculiar tinge of Prussian conservatism consisted mainly in the idea that the state stood like an impartial, objective force, as the guardian of peace and justice above the strife of particular private and group interests, whereas English and American political philosophy, like that of the Liberals and Socialists in Germany, is inclined to a more realistic view. It cannot, however, be denied that the Conservative idea of the state had its grandiose aspects and that it had created in Germany, and particularly in Prussia, an ethic of public service of high quality.

The National Socialists, far from re-establishing this political creed and this code of political morality, have torn down and perverted every one of its tenets.

The elevation of the "community of the people" (*Volksgemeinschaft*) to the rank of the ultimate ethical value sharply contradicts the Christian doctrine.[17] It also leads to the abnegation of the humanitarian tradition, which constitutes a main element in Western civilization. This cult of the ethnic community is by no means identical with the deification of the state.[18] It is much farther removed from Western tradition than that. For, the *Volksgemeinschaft*, unlike the state, comprises only those inhabitants

[17] See, for instance, A. Rosenberg, *Der Mythus des 20. Jahrhunderts*, p. 486, where this is candidly stated.

[18] See Rosenberg, *op. cit.*, pp. 496 ff.; he states this very clearly. Hegel's doctrine of the state which had become dominant in Germany had resulted in a separation of the state from the organic body of the people. According to Rosenberg, the state is not an end, but "only a means for the preservation of the people." The authority of the people (*Volkheit*) is higher than that of the state. "Anybody who does not acknowledge this is an enemy of the people, *and be it the state itself* [italics mine]. That is the situation today."

of the state's territory who can prove their "aryan descent"; and on the other hand, it comprises citizens of other sovereign, national states, who are or claim to be "Germans" in the ethnic sense. Practically speaking, the baptized "Jew" Stahl, who about the middle of the nineteenth century systematized the doctrine of constitutional monarchism and thereby furnished the Prussian Conservatives with a political theory, would be treated as a stranger and outcast, while some of our outstanding American generals would be claimed for the German "ethnic community."

Furthermore, even among those who because of "aryan" descent qualify as members of the *Volksgemeinschaft*, there exists a division into the privileged "élite" of the party comrades and the ordinary mass of *Volksgenossen;* again a principle foreign to the Conservative tradition which recognizes at the utmost distinctions by birth.[19]

The leadership principle, being the very antithesis to the principle of legality, means the abnegation of the rule-of-law state. For, the leader, being the incarnation of the ethnic community, is the fountain of all law; unlike the kings and princes of the past, he is bound neither by law nor custom; he is "always right" because of his personal superior intuition and gift of leadership.[20] The content

[19] It is curiously little known that one of the disqualifications for membership in the NSDAP was former membership in a Freemason's order. This is another deviation from the Prussian tradition. Freemasons contributed greatly to the unification of the Reich and several members of the House of Hohenzollern have been Freemasons. The Nazis' antagonism to Freemasonry is a consequence of the "deification" of the people's community, which does not tolerate any other organization claiming loyalty. Anti-Masonry appealed probably to many of the middle class elements who found themselves excluded from the lodges; it also harmonized with anti-Semitism as the German lodges had always rejected anti-Semitism.

[20] See the discussion by Hans Gerth, "The Nazi Party: Its Leadership and Composition," *American Journal of Sociology*, Vol. XLV, No. 4, pp. 517–541.

of the law and the course of its administration is unhampered by any supra-political principles, such as the ideas of natural rights and justice. Nor are the courts held to adhere to the letter of the law. The only guiding line in the administration of the law is the interest and welfare of the *Volksgemeinschaft*. That is, the principle of "formal" justice which has been one of the mainstays of the Western states and which was particularly honored in pre-Nazi Germany [21] has been abandoned.

Since in the last instance the leader alone determines what is the "welfare of the *Volksgemeinschaft*," adjusting his revelations to the demands of constantly changing political situations, this new doctrine of law inevitably leads to a practice of judicial decisions determined by political and administrative expediency rather than by the idea of justice or by the prescriptions of positive law. The ultimate result is complete abolition of the safeguards of life, liberty, and property.[22]

The organization and institutions of the state have of course been preserved. Offices, and even officials of the pre-Nazi regime, have in many instances been taken over into the Third Reich; but their function has been changed. From being agents of the supreme secular authority, they have been demoted to the role of servants of the party. It

---

[21] There was no lack of critical discussion; the attacks on the formal jurisprudence by the *Freie Rechtsschule* and other groups were led by very able scholars, and it is one of the ironies of the Third Reich that jurists who had been the pupils of the leaders in the sociological schools of jurisprudence have become the defenders and exegetes of the Nazi doctrine of law.

[22] For details see Ernst Fraenkel, *The Dual State* (New York, 1941). Fraenkel maintains that this decomposition of the rule-of-law state has stopped short only where the nature of a capitalistic economy demands calculability of the law. He presents a wealth of evidence from court decisions and opinions of party dignitaries which give an excellent idea of the true nature of the Third Reich.

is the party or, as the Nazis like to put it, the movement, which generates and proclaims the political directives—lastly of course always on authority of the leader. The party thus becomes the real power, and the interests and purposes of the party the true aims of political life. Any deviation from or opposition to the protean, constantly changing party directives is heresy.[23]

For all practical purposes this means even the destruction of the "community of the people" and the subjection of the intimidated population to the willful rule of the party oligarchy. The condition of mutual trust and confidence which is indispensable in any true community is difficult enough to create and maintain in large and highly complex modern societies. While in smaller and simpler societies one may rely to a large extent on a natural, spontaneous sense of solidarity, such sentiments have to be reinforced in the "Great Society" by certain institutions which give to the individual a sense of personal security and protect him against arbitrary use of political power. What we call "civil rights" in Western democracies is

[23] Hitler's regime is a case of what Max Weber has called "charismatic leadership"; perhaps not a pure case, but one which comes very close to it. The essence of it is that the leader owes his authority to his followers' belief in his extraordinary gifts and powers. Charismatic leadership is the antithesis of forms of authority which derive their legitimation from a sacred tradition or from a rational legal order. The distinction helps in understanding the difference between dictatorship in the original sense of the term and the leadership principle. A genuine dictator may derive his authority either from tradition or from constitutional law; he acts as an agent of the people in emergencies, having temporary powers conferred upon him, without intention of making his regime permanent. The distinction may be further elaborated by pointing out that a dictator, while he may have the support of a certain party, does not create his personal "following"—if he did so he would cease to be a genuine dictator. The charismatic leader on the other hand is unthinkable without a personal following which is his own creation. Failure to see these fundamental differences is responsible for much confusion in political thinking.

largely a set of devices to organize a community-like solidarity in the Great Society.[24] Under the Hitler regime

[24] On the contrast between community and society, see Ferdinand Tönnies, "Gemeinschaft und Gesellschaft," *Handwoerterbuch der Soziologie 1931,* a late statement of Tönnies' theory. This article is incorporated in Charles P. Loomis' translation of Tönnies' main work (F. Tönnies, *Fundamental Concepts of Sociology, Gemeinschaft und Gesellschaft,* New York, 1940). The *Gemeinschafts*-idea, or idea of community as a basic element in social life, which in our age is in danger of being lost and the restoration of which is the foremost task of political and cultural reform, had been taken absolutely seriously by large masses of Hitler's early and later followers. It was of course an old idea, the history of which cannot be traced in this study. Small circles in the prewar generation, e. g., in the early youth movement, had tried by exemplary ways of living to restore the communal principle in the Great Society. The postwar period saw a large-scale revival of the youth movement and numerous other experiments in communal life. From these circles, the idea was diffused into political movements; particularly the "Jungdeutsche Orden" and various branches of the "Voelkische" movement adopted the idea.

It is important that all these early *Gemeinschafts*-movements were thinking in terms of small and autonomous groups as the nuclei of the new order of the nation. The position of their leaders was very unstable; they had to give continuous evidence of their ability as they could not rely on organized administrative staffs to enforce their will on the group. The groups themselves were unstable in membership and cohesion; frequent secessions and regroupings were characteristic events in the history of the youth movement. The Hitler Youth, which adopted the terminology and some of the symbolisms of the youth movement had an entirely different character. The regimentation and uniformalization of all activities, down to the smallest local units, by the Reich leader, whose authority was backed by the Fuehrer and the entire party organization and lastly by the Gestapo, formed a contrast in principles to the loose and informal organization of the youth movement.

The difference between the National Socialists' idea of *Volksgemeinschaft* and the community ideas of the earlier movements can be defined as the difference between a genuine primary-group conception of community and a behavioristic conception of a large-scale organization for the achievement of uniformity in conduct by compulsion and training. From the point of view of the ruling minority of Nazi party leaders, such a pseudo-community was quite sufficient; absolute obedience to the leader and his underlings, oppression of all dissenting or antagonistic movements were, from the Nazis' point of view, essential conditions of successful rearmament and preparation for the coming war.

such solidarity was allegedly restored in Germany. In reality, fear, suspicion, distrust, and insincerity tended to poison all human relations, even those of the more intimate kind. For, nobody could rely any longer on the courts to protect him against attacks on his political or moral reputation, on his honor, his property, or his life and liberty. Not even party members were exempt from this insecurity.[25] It is in this sense that the Nazis undermined not only the state but also the community of the nation. Perhaps this condition was not quite unwelcome to the inner circle of the party since it seemed to prevent any organized resistance and made it easier to draw the nation into the war of revenge which should lead to the establishment of the Nazi order in the world.

Like all political parties, the NSDAP had an urban origin. It found its first foothold in Bavarian and Thuringian cities, and when it spread to north Germany, it was again in cities that the first locals were organized; and the cities remained the main field of the party's activities for some time.

Yet during the second period of its history, after Hitler's return to public life, the party became more rural.[26] In the cities its growth was checked,[27] mainly through the existence of a very firm bloc of Social Democratic and Communist labor votes, while in some rural areas it obtained strong majorities, in many villages even a virtual monopoly. The membership also became more and more rural; even in the cities a conspicuously large proportion of the members had a rural or small town background.

[25] See John Brown Mason, "The Judicial System of the Nazi Party," *The American Political Science Review* (February, 1944), pp. 89–95.

[26] See, for instance, *Nationalsozialistische Monatschefte, 1930,* No. 1, pp. 34 ff., and Heiden, *op. cit.,* pp. 252 ff.

[27] Werner Stephan, Grenzen des Nationalsozialistischen Vormarsches; *Zeitschrift fuer Politik* (December, 1931).

Consequently, if one wants to understand the reasons for its final success, one should study the Nazi movement in its rural strongholds.

II

POLITICAL PARTIES AND ELECTIONS
IN SCHLESWIG-HOLSTEIN BEFORE
THE FIRST WORLD WAR

ABOUT 1930 the rural areas of Schleswig-Holstein had become one of the strongholds of the Nazi party. Since the political development in the region followed the general pattern of the Reich in all essential respects and since the region comprises various types of rural society which are also found in other parts of the Reich, Schleswig-Holstein seems to offer a good opportunity for an intensive regional case study of political parties and movements during the fateful period which preceded the Nazi regime. The limitation of the study to a region which is well known to the investigator in all its relevant aspects has certain advantages as compared with a nation-wide study.

The present paper deals with the development of political opinion in Schleswig-Holstein from its incorporation into the German Reich to the First World War. Space restrictions necessitate a limitation to the survey and brief interpretation of election results. This chapter should be regarded as an introduction to the two following studies rather than as an independent paper.

The duchies of Schleswig and Holstein belonged to those territories of the former German Empire which were annexed by Prussia after the war with Austria in 1866. Their relation to each other, to the Danish State, and to the German Confederation (*Deutscher Bund*) was one of the anomalies in the world of modern centralized states which had survived from the age of feudalism.

During the first half of the nineteenth century the predominant opinion in the duchies demanded with increasing definiteness incorporation into a new German Empire; yet the solution of Bismarck's by which the duchies were reduced to the status of a Prussian province was not what the Schleswig-Holstein patriots had wanted. Nor were they satisfied with the "Little Germany" under Prussian domination which emerged from the war of 1870–1871.

Consequently, during the first years after the annexation and the reconstitution of the Empire there was a great deal of opposition to the new regime. This came to a clear expression in the first elections for the German Reichstag. Seven out of nine delegates belonged to the opposition parties and no Conservative candidate was elected. Even the National Liberals, who won 119 out of 382 seats in the Reichstag, obtained only one out of nine in Schleswig-Holstein (Table 1).

Gradually, however, the opposition receded as the wealthier farmers and the upper classes in the cities became reconciled to the new regime, a process which was greatly facilitated by the rather rapid improvement of the economic conditions. The larger German market was opened to the cattle farmers of Holstein and Schleswig; Kiel was developed as a large naval base; and the region participated in the general economic upswing of the Reich. The elections of 1878 saw six Conservatives and only three Progressives plus one candidate of the *Protestpartei* elected. The next elections, in 1881, however, brought victory again to the opposition parties. This condition prevailed in most elections until 1912, when the Progressives and Social Democrats obtained all seats, except one from an election district at the Danish border which had been

TABLE 1. REICHSTAG MEMBERS ELECTED IN SCHLESWIG-HOLSTEIN

Party	1871	1874	1877	1878	1881	1884	1887	1890	1893	1898	1903	1907	1912
Konservative	—	—	1	1	1	1	1	1	1	—	—	—	—
Freikonservative	1	—	—	1	—	1	—	—	2	2	—	—	—
Nationalliberale	1	4	5	4	—	2	3	1	2	2	1	2	—
Fortschrittspartei and Freisinnige (Progressives)	4	2	3	3	7	4	4	5	2	2	2	5	7
Social Democrats	—	2	—	—	—	1	1	2	2	2	5	2	2
Particularists	2	—	—	—	—	—	—	—	—	—	—	—	—
Protest party	1	1	1	1	—	—	—	—	—	—	—	—	1
Danes	—	—	—	—	2	1	1	1	1	1	1	—	1
Anti-Semites	—	—	—	—	—	—	—	—	—	1	1	1	—
Total	9	9	10	10	10	10	10	10	10	10	10	10	10

Sources: Monatshefte zur Statistik des Deutschen Reiches 1874, 1875, 1879, 1882, 1885, 1887, 1890. Vierteljahrshefte zur Statistik des Deutschen Reiches 1893, 1900, 1903, 1904, 1907. Statistik des Deutschen Reiches Band 250.

held since 1881 by a representative of the pro-Danish party (Table 1).

The elections in this period were decided by an absolute majority; consequently, there were often run-off elections in which competing parties had to compromise on the stronger candidate. Therefore, a better picture of the constellations of political opinion can be obtained from the original elections (Table 2).

These elections show since 1890 a strong and increasing following of the Social Democrats, who at various elections obtained from 32.2 to 44.3 per cent of the total vote. Their rise was only partly a consequence of industrialization; as early as 1898 about 30.7 per cent of the Social Democratic votes in Schleswig-Holstein were cast in rural communities. On the other hand, 22.5 per cent of the total rural votes were Social Democratic. That was the highest score the party made in any of the provinces of Prussia; the highly industrialized province of Saxony ranked next with 21.5 per cent; then followed Brandenburg with 20.4 per cent, Hesse with 18.5, Hannover with 14.5, East Prussia with 12.6, and Silesia with 12.4 per cent. In Schleswig-Holstein the Social Democrats had their main rural strongholds in those election districts which were either close to large cities or had a predominance of large estates and large farms.[28] This was a result of the decadence of the old-style patriarchal labor relations, which was quite advanced in the larger commercialized agricultural enterprises in the region.[29]

---

[28] Schleswig-Eckernfoerde, Kiel-Rendsburg-Ploen, North and South Dithmarschen, Pinneberg-Segeberg, Altona-Stormarn, Lauenburg.

[29] Wuebbena, "Ueber die Arbeitsverhaeltnisse in der Provinz Schleswig-Holstein," *Arbeiten der Landwirtschaftskammer für die Provinz Schleswig-Holstein*, Heft 2 (Kiel, 1900). A. Grunenberg, "Die Landarbeiter in der Provinz Schleswig-Holstein und Hannover" in Max Weber (ed.), *Die Landarbeiter in den Evangelischen Gebieten Norddeutschlands. Eine Ein-*

TABLE 2. PRIMARY REICHSTAG ELECTIONS IN SCHLESWIG-HOLSTEIN, 1871 TO 1912, IN PER CENT OF TOTAL VOTE

Party	1871	1874	1877	1878	1881	1884	1887	1890	1893	1898	1903	1907	1912
Konservative	9.1	0.1	8.2	16.2	20.2	6.0	5.7	4.2	4.6	1.2[1]	1.4[1]	—	5.4[1]
Freikonservative	4.4	6.1	3.0	7.7	1.4	3.3	6.3	7.4	8.2	9.4	9.3	5.0	3.0
Nationalliberale	16.1	20.6	29.1	20.4	10.7	28.0	29.4	19.8	12.2	14.5	14.3	15.1	14.0
Fortschrittspartei and Freisinnige (Progressives)	24.9	15.4	15.4	23.7	44.9	34.2	30.4	29.2	26.3	22.0	21.2	31.8	29.2
Social Democrats	12.6	32.8	29.0	19.6	11.2	17.9	21.5	32.2	37.7	38.8	44.3	38.9	40.4
Particularists	7.9	10.2	3.7	1.5	—	—	—	—	—	—	—	—	—
Protest party	20.6	14.5	11.5	10.8	—	—	—	—	—	—	—	—	—
Danes	—	—	—	—	11.4	10.5	6.6	7.1	7.1	7.4	6.0	5.3	5.5
Anti-Semites	—	—	—	—	—	—	—	0.0	1.5	6.3	2.8	2.8[2]	1.8
Center and others	4.4	0.2	0.1	0.1	0.2	0.1	0.1	0.1	2.4	0.4	0.7	1.1	0.7
Votes cast in per cent of persons entitled to vote	42.9	61.8	65.0	63.2	54.0	58.4	76.3	74.6		72.8	76.2	85.8	85.2

[1] Including Bund der Landwirte.
[2] Including various groups.
Sources: Monatshefte zur Statistik des Deutschen Reiches 1874, 1875, 1879, 1882, 1885, 1887, 1890.
Vierteljahrshefte zur Statistik des Deutschen Reiches 1893, 1900, 1903, 1904, 1907.
Statistik des Deutschen Reiches, Band 250.

The striking success of the Social Democrats in the Reichstag elections of 1903, when they obtained 44.3 per cent of the votes, led to a coalition of the left-wing Liberal parties in Schleswig-Holstein. The debates which preceded the formation of a Liberal cartel emphasized particularly the need for better party organization. It was pointed out that the middle classes,[30] which formed the main support of the Liberal parties, had been lagging behind in efficient economic interest organization, as compared with the large landowners who had formed the Farmers' League (*Bund der Landwirte*) and with the workers with their powerful unions. It was proposed that the loose organization of the Liberal parties, hitherto under volunteer personnel recruited from the ranks of prominent citizens, be "streamlined" by a more formal organization in local associations and by employment of a paid full-time party secretary for the entire province; in other words, the first steps towards bureaucratization of the liberal parties would be taken.

What were the economic and political interests that drove the middle classes of small businessmen and small manufacturers, the educated middle class, and the small farmers into the camp of Progressivism (*Freisinn*)? There was a basic attitude of liberalism to begin with; furthermore, certain concrete issues led to a clarification of political inclinations within the middle classes: they were opposed to protective tariffs on grain and feedstuff because the owners of large estates benefited by them chiefly; they

---

zeldarstellung nach den Erhebungen des Evangelisch-sozialen Kongresses, 2. Heft (Tuebingen, 1899). F. Grossmann, "Die Laendlichen Arbeiterverhaeltnisse in der Provinz Schleswig-Holstein," usw. in *Schriften des Vereins für Sozialpolitik,* LIV (Leipzig, 1892). Max Sering, *Die Deutsche Landwirtschaft unter Volks-und Weltwirtschaftlichen Gesichtspunkten* (Berlin, 1932).

[30] To be more specific: the *"Mittelstand,"* that is, mainly the smaller farmers and the petty bourgeoisie or *"Kleinbuergertum."*

were also opposed to industrial protective tariffs because these facilitated the formation of cartels in the large scale industries and thereby imposed a burden on the industrial and commercial middle class.[31]

The educated or intellectual groups were more inclined to think in terms of political principles: they had been repelled by Bismarck's handling of the *"Kulturkampf,"* i. e., the conflict with the Roman Catholic Church and the Center party. They demanded an expansion of the rights of the Reichstag and of the Prussian *Landtag;* they were opposed to anti-Semitism; they also objected to the armament policy, partly for financial and partly for ethical reasons.

And yet, one can, in the ideology of the progressive Liberals in the region, discern certain attitudes and sentiments which later on facilitated the conversion of broad masses of middle class elements to National Socialism: There was a combination of anti-capitalistic, anti-plutocratic sentiments with anti-imperialistic attitudes, and of an emphatic rejection of proletarian Socialism with an attitude of social solidarity that favored progressive labor legislation or *Sozialpolitik.*

Large-scale manufacturing was concentrated in a few cities; there were still many small and medium-sized plants even in the metropolitan cities. On the other hand, the farmers were not, like the large landowners, tied to the Conservative parties by protectionism; the Liberal attitude was still quite far spread. The prospects of a Liberal victory in the Reichstag elections were therefore favorable, especially if an alliance between the Progressive cartel and the National Liberals could be formed.[32]

The elections of 1907 and 1912 resulted in complete

[31] *Kieler Zeitung,* February 14, 1905, morning edition.
[32] *Kieler Zeitung,* April 25, 1905, evening edition.

victories of the Liberal parties over the Conservative; in
the latter elections the Progressives controlled all election districts except two which had been firmly in the hands
of the Social Democrats for some time.

Even in those years one could speak of a "two-front
war" of Liberalism; if the left-wing Liberals could score
such an overwhelming success in 1912, it was because of
skillful exploitation of tactical chances: they would join
forces with the Social Democrats in the run-off elections
in districts with a predominance of large estates, while in
medium or small farm districts they would gain the support of the National Liberals and Conservatives.

The upper classes in city and country remained
predominantly National Liberal and Free-Conservative.
Their political attitudes were those characteristic of the
upper classes in all recently annexed Protestant provinces
of Prussia; they were basically Conservative and yet un-
willing to betray their political tradition, particularly their
participation in the Liberal movement for national unity.
In this way the *Nationalliberale* and the *Freikonservative*
parties became the representatives of the Conservative
groups.

The gradual shift of the lower and middle classes,
precisely in the years of economic prosperity, towards Progressivism (*Freisinn*) and Social Democracy was an expression of opposition to a political system which in Prussia deprived these classes of important civil rights, while
in the Reich it drained their purses by increasing indirect
taxes in order to meet the growing financial burden of
armament, at the same time rejecting the reform of income and inheritance taxes. The shift was also an expression of animosity against the increasing political and economic power of big business and of dissatisfaction with a
foreign trade policy that favored the large-scale enterprises

and did not adequately consider the interests of cattle and dairy farming in the region. Finally, a particular regional note of discontent entered into the motivations because of conditions in the border districts where the Prussian administration succeeded in antagonizing rather than reconciling the Danish-speaking minority.

Schleswig-Holstein thus represented a type of political opinion more characteristic of northwest Germany than of the east; and, as in other new Prussian regions, the period before the First World War concluded with a complete victory in the elections for the democratic wing of Liberalism, the aims of which were the expansion of the rights of parliament and democratization of Prussia in general.

The impending political clash between the rising movement for democracy and the forces in power was postponed by the First World War. The collapse of the imperial regime in 1918 resulted in the establishment of parliamentary democratic government. This fulfillment of democratic demands came almost without struggle. It was the second time in German history that this happened, and that was unfortunate, because political rights and institutions that have been received as gifts from fate are not likely to be held as high as those for which brave men have fought and died.

III

THE POLITICAL MOVEMENTS AMONG THE RURAL PEOPLE IN SCHLESWIG-HOLSTEIN, 1918 TO 1932

In the change of public opinion which led to the breakdown of democracy in Germany the political opinion of the rural population has been a factor of great importance.[33] In the Reichstag elections in the summer of 1932, certain rural sections voted almost unanimously for the Nazi party, and only in rural communities did the Nazis obtain such large majorities at that time. Foremost among these rural strongholds of the Hitler movement was the border-region Schleswig-Holstein. Here in the Reichstag elections of 1930 the National Socialists had obtained the largest percentage of votes (27 per cent) of any election district. Two years later, in the Reichstag elections of July, 1932, Schleswig-Holstein was the only election district in the whole Reich where the National Socialists gained an absolute majority (51 per cent of the total vote). This represented one of the most surprising developments; for, in the years before and after the First World War, this region had been a stronghold of the Liberal and Democratic parties. Even the Conservatives were of a rather liberal denomination. An attempt to understand this sudden conversion to a political creed seemingly in contradic-

[33] Cf. Carl J. Friedrich, "The Agricultural Basis of Emotional Nationalism," *Public Opinion Quarterly*, Vol. 1, No. 1 (1937), pp. 50 ff.

tion to all political tradition, even to the temperament of the Schleswig-Holstein people, necessitates a comprehensive study of political parties and elections in Schleswig-Holstein from the foundation of the second German Empire in 1871 to the critical summer of 1932.[34] The analysis has been concentrated, however, on the postwar period and the rural population. The study of rural political opinion encounters peculiar obstacles since farmers and agricultural laborers, and even great landlords, are not apt to express their thoughts in speeches or writing. The rural newspapers, never a very true expression of the sentiments and opinions of farmers,[35] represent them less today than ever. The most immediate indicator, and at the same time the only one which lends itself to quantitative analysis, is the record of the balloting in political elections.

The limitation of this study to one region well known to the author has the advantage that all relevant aspects of social life could be taken into consideration. This study was, therefore, based upon a detailed analysis of election results by administrative districts (*Kreise*) and incorporated towns, and, for two elections, by communities (*Landgemeinden* and *Städte*) and subregions. The election results have been correlated with various indices of the socio-economic structure of the population; finally, an inquiry has been made into the influence of changes in economic conditions, especially the depression from 1929 onwards, upon the political attitudes of the rural people.

[34] Limitation of the study to this period is necessary because the elections of July 31, 1932, offered the last opportunity for a really free expression of public opinion.

[35] This explains the scarcity of studies on this subject. André Siegfried, *Tableau Politique de la France de l'Ouest sous la Troisiéme République* (Paris, 1919), deserves to be mentioned as the classical work in the field. Arthur N. Holcombe, *Political Parties and Elections* (New York, 1926), is also of basic importance. The German literature does not contain any studies comparable to these in scope and thoroughness.

Schleswig-Holstein lends itself particularly well to this kind of analysis because of its ecological structure. Since it comprises certain typical structure situations of society found in larger sections of north Germany, the conclusions derived from this study possess a more general validity.

Schleswig-Holstein is a border province in more than the ordinary sense: although the German-Danish border cuts across the narrow peninsula from west to east, there runs from north to south through its eastern part the important line of demarcation between the old Germanic and the previously Slavic "colonial" regions of Germany.[36] In view of a recently advanced theory about the background of Nazism [37] this fact deserves to be emphasized. Schleswig-Holstein combines, therefore, the structure of rural society elements of western and eastern Germany. Furthermore, the three major physiographic zones which divide the peninsula in a north-south direction—the coastal marshes in the west, the rolling sandy *Geest* in the middle, and the Baltic hill zone in the east—represent parts of the major physiographic regions of the north German plain. Both the marshes and the eastern hill zones differ considerably in their social structure from the *Geest*.

The North Sea marshes extend from the Netherlands into Denmark, presenting, on the whole, the same social conditions as in Schleswig-Holstein. Geologically a recent formation, the marshlands of Schleswig-Holstein have been reclaimed and cultivated, during historical times, by settlers from the southern part of the *Geest* and also by Frisian and Dutch colonists. An extremely fertile soil, the coastal location, and political freedom have combined to

---

[36] Paul von Hedemann-Heespen, "Ueber Gutsherrschaft und Bauern an der Ostküste Schleswig-Holsteins," *Zeitschrift für Schleswig-Holsteinische Geschichte* (1913), pp. 507 ff.

[37] Goetz A. Briefs, "Limes Germanicus—Bridge and Frontier," *The Review of Politics*, Vol. 1 (1939), pp. 261, 444.

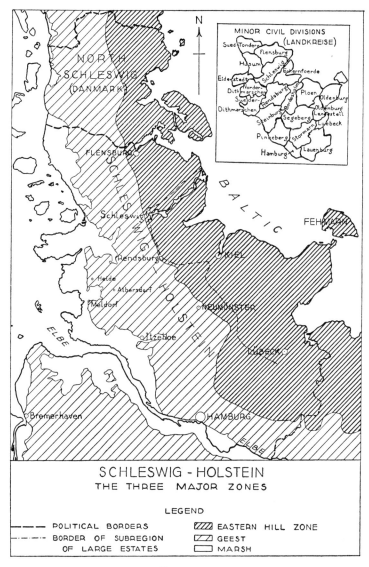

SCHLESWIG - HOLSTEIN
THE THREE MAJOR ZONES

LEGEND

——— POLITICAL BORDERS	▨ EASTERN HILL ZONE
—··—··— BORDER OF SUBREGION	▨ GEEST
OF LARGE ESTATES	▭ MARSH

FIGURE 1

foster the development of a rural society of peculiar structure. The territories of Dithmarschen and Eiderstedt had succeeded in preserving the ancient liberties of Germanic freeholders into modern times. Never were they forced into serfdom. They retained all the essential features of self-government until the loose connection with the Danish crown was replaced by the more centralized and bureaucratic rule of Prussia. Positions of authority and public offices were held by a class of big farmers which in wealth, enterprise, and political status was comparable to the peasant aristocracies in Scandinavian countries. Having engaged in various specialties of production for distant markets as early as the sixteenth century, they began to specialize in raising beef cattle for the English market in the nineteenth century, financing this business by a farmer-owned bank. Wheat and, in more recent times, produce of truck gardens are the next important products. Accustomed to specialized production for distant markets—that is, to a kind of agriculture which involves a great deal of financial acumen and shrewdness in business transactions—the marsh farmers have acquired much of the mentality of commercial entrepreneurs, though still remaining passionately attached to the land and to their occupation. Since cattle grazing does not impose heavy regular work on the farmer, these big farmers often engage in commercial enterprises or even in the practice of the law. Consequently, they are more than is usual in the case of farmers available for public office and political life. Even the next stratum, that of the less wealthy farmers who perform some manual labor, live and conduct themselves very much like gentlemen. Both strata are thus related by kinship and intermarriage with the professions, the clergy, and the civil service; even before the First World War the men often held commissions in the army reserve.

The large farms are operated with comparatively few hired hands who are recruited from a quite distinct class of poor people: small farmers, cottagers, and even landless workers who dwell in separate settlements along the sea-levees and the escarpment of the *Geest*. Rural society in the marshes is thus highly stratified and can be characterized even for the period under consideration as a peasant aristocracy.[38]

The eastern hill zone of Holstein was colonized by Germans in the eleventh and twelfth centuries. Here, however, the Germans found part of the land occupied by Slavic invaders who were subdued in a prolonged struggle. As usual, in cases of conquest, a class of noble landlords was established, which in the course of time ceded more and more of its military and administrative functions to the officers of the crown and developed more and more into a class of large-scale agriculturists. This process, however, was not carried to such extremes as in certain other parts of northeast Germany; the displacement of peasants or their reduction to the state of landless laborers was checked and a fairly well-to-do and very stable class of tenant farmers was preserved. Besides these, there are communities of owner-farmers interspersed with the large estates.

This zone reaches its northern limit in the southeastern part of Angeln, the peninsula north of the river Schlei. Here the majority of the population consists of farmers. The stratification is quite distinct, depending on the size of the farm. The people here are probably of Scandinavian origin; they are perhaps more given to things of the mind and the soul than the marshdwellers. The density of churches is symptomatic of a relatively strong religiosity

[38] Similar conditions are found on the Isle of Fehmarn in the Baltic which is said to have been settled by emigrants from the marshes.

(which is utterly absent in the marshes). The entire zone has highly fertile, mostly loamy soils which make it an excellent country for wheat, rye, and other grains. A peculiar rotation of crops providing for considerable livestock and dairy production was adopted here at an early date. In Angeln the system is particularly well balanced and it has enabled the farmers to withstand the severe depression of the late 1920's far better than any other group of farmers in Schleswig-Holstein.

The *Geest* had been a poor and economically retarded section until artificial fertilizer came into use at the end of the nineteenth century. This proverbial poor man's land had never been very attractive to the nobility. Consequently, the large majority of *Geest* peasants have always remained freeholders, subject, however, to the territorial overlords (*Landesherren*) to whom they owed services and quitrents. There has developed a flourishing industry of cattle breeding which furnishes young steers and heifers for the grazing farms in the marshes. Dairying and the products of the chicken yard provide a constant flow of cash, so that the *Geest* farmer is less in need of production credits than the marsh farmer or wheat farmer of the hill zone. However, because of dependence on the beef cattle market, the distribution of economic risks is not as favorable as on the mixed farms of the hill zone. Owing to the almost complete absence of large estates and to the scarcity of really rich farmers, there is much less stratification on the *Geest* than in any of the other zones. The separation of *Gut* and *Dorf* (estate and village), which in the eastern zone symbolizes the class structure, and the isolation of the big farmers on their scattered homesteads, which is characteristic of the marsh, are not found here; the *Geest* is a region of peasant villages. The *Geest* farmer has caught less of the spirit of capitalistic enterprise than the marsh farmer; he is in mentality and in habits still more of a real peasant. He is looked upon by the marsh farmers very much as the Southern hill-billy or redneck is looked upon by the planters. Because of the small size of the farm, the owner and his family perform all the operations in the fields and stables, aided only by a few hired men and maids who come from families of like or similar social status. Consequently, class distinctions are scarcely noticeable, and a spirit of neighborliness and true community prevails.

It was here on the *Geest* that the Nazi party in July, 1932, scored its greatest successes; if the National Socialist percentages of the total vote in each community were plotted on a map, the overwhelming majority of those communities in which the National Socialists received 80 per cent or more of the total vote would be located within the *Geest* zone. The National Socialist percentages decline towards the east and the west, while the percentages of the *Deutschnationale Volkspartei* (Conservative) [39] and of the Social Democratic and Communist parties tend to be lower on the *Geest* and higher in the other two zones. Thus, it is permissible to assume that the socio-economic zones are largely coincident with the political zones. This distribution of the rural vote of the major parties in the summer of 1932 was quite representative of rural conditions in the Reich in general. Wherever the community structure resembled those of the *Geest,* at least in Protestant territory, there was a stronghold of

[39] The *Deutschnationale Volkspartei* (DNVP) is often referred to as the Conservatives. The *Deutsche Volkspartei* (DVP), which was Stresemann's party, was the successor to the old National Liberal party. The *Deutsche Demokratische Partei* (DDP) was the successor to the old Progressive party. The Social Democratic party (SPD) and the Communist party of Germany (KPD) were major parties, of course.

National Socialism, while in areas of pronounced class differentiation, the Conservatives and the two Marxist parties maintained their positions better.[40]

The political atmosphere is not created merely by propaganda and by the formation of individual opinion; it rather originates in groups and movements of a more or less distinct, more or less organized, character. In the period of German history with which we are concerned, the close connection of organized groups, representing particular interests, with the political parties was one of the outstanding features of the political structure. Our study therefore deals not only with political ideologies and party organizations but also with the farmers' organizations, their platforms, and tactics. On the other hand, the competition of the political parties for support from these organizations forms another theme in this study.

The political "atmosphere" consists of various layers, or one may say, of various air currents, some of them being of a very short-lived nature, some more constant, and others very persistent. There are first the currents of the day, the short squalls and breezes, caused by some incident or some action of a political leader; then there are the more persistent traditions of party adherence; and finally, certain very constant basic attitudes which survive even a complete change in the constellation of political parties. These basic attitudes are partly determined by interests which in turn are conditioned mostly by the occupations and industries of the population; but there are others which are determined by historical events, by past experiences such as victory or defeat in war. One of these basic attitudes in Schleswig-Holstein was developed by

[40] This statement is based upon the analysis of election results by *Kreise* and *Gemeinden* previously referred to. See also Ch. IV.

the annexation to Prussia in 1866 and the subsequent policy of the Prussian administration. Similar anti-Prussian attitudes were present in other regions of the Empire and resurged after the downfall of the imperial regime. We shall see how this factor played finally into the hands of the Hitler movement.

Turning now to the determination of party preferences by occupational and industrial interests, we find, during the period 1918–1932, three large social groups as the main channels of political currents in Schleswig-Holstein:

1. The large landowner class together with its adherents among the big farmers and the bourgeoisie; they formed the main support of conservatism.

2. The urban and rural middle classes, i. e., in the rural districts mainly the small farmers and the semi-proletarian cottagers (*Kätner*), along with certain groups of the agricultural laborers who in the beginning of the period were leaning towards liberalism, though finally they furnished the main support to the National Socialist movement.

3. The industrial labor class, reinforced by segments of the salaried-employee class and, in the rural areas, by the cottagers and landless agricultural workers, especially in areas of large estates (*Güter*) and large farms. These were the nucleus of the Social Democratic party and, at a later stage, furnished recruits for the Communists.

After the end of the First World War, political power rested for some time with the second and third groups. The overwhelming majority of votes in Schleswig-Holstein in the elections to the constitutional national assembly went to the Liberal and Social Democratic parties. Old anti-Prussian feelings combined with more temporary ripples of political sentiment produced this attitude.

Apparently, in the rural areas, the Social Democratic party had succeeded in gaining votes beyond the circle of the rural proletariat. Many farmers, and especially those engaging in cattle breeding and dairying, had been in opposition to the imperial government since 1917, owing to the restrictions on private initiative in farm management imposed by measures of war economy. Thus, they supported for some time the parties of the Weimar coalition as the adversaries of the overthrown regime. Fear of radical socialism also may have contributed to bringing about an alliance with the moderate wing of the "Left." However, when the new ruling groups continued the measures of war economy in order to secure cheap food supplies for the urban population, the chronic attitude of opposition which many farmers maintained turned immediately against the supporters of the new regime. The new Prussia did not succeed in really winning the sympathy of the Schleswig-Holstein farmer class—being, as a socialist representative called it, the rock of the revolution, the most important stronghold of the Social Democratic party. While anti-Prussian particularist movements had formerly looked for allies among the Social Democrats and Liberals, they now associated with the adversaries of these.

Since conservatism in Schleswig-Holstein immediately after the war had lost almost the last remnant of its influence even in the country (the *Deutschnationale Volkspartei* received only 11 per cent of the votes in rural sections), the *Bauernverein* [41] movement came into being and for some time gained great importance as the rallying point of the farmers' opposition. The first *Bauernverein* had been founded in the spring of 1918 in North Schleswig in order to represent the economic interests of

[41] The German titles of the various farmers' associations are retained. Their German titles and English equivalents are as follows: *Bauernverein,* Farmers' Union; *Landbund,* Agrarian League; and *Bauernbund,* Peasants' League.

the cattle-raising farmers on the *Geest* in the contest with the war economy agencies. The locals of the *Bauernverein,* which since June, 1918, had been united as *Bauernverein des Nordens,* spread in 1918 and 1919 over the entire *Geest.* They also gained a foothold in Dithmarschen and North Friesland and in the farm sections of the eastern hill zone, although here the resistance of the Conservatives was more effective than in farming sections without any large estates. This conflict arose immediately when it looked as if the *Bauernverein* were going to be an organization of *all* the farmers of Schleswig-Holstein and that it would replace the old conservative organization of farmers, the *Landbund,* in which the owners of large estates had always been the leaders.[42]

Politically, the *Bauernverein* made contact at first with the Liberals, i. e., with the *Deutsche Demokratische Partei,* later with the *Deutsche Volkspartei.* These connections, as well as the contacts with the Catholic *Bauernvereine* in Westphalia and in the Ermland,[43] were used in the *Landbund* and by the Conservatives to discredit the Schleswig-Holstein *Bauernverein.* The leaders of the *Bauernverein* themselves seem to have regarded their connection with the Liberals merely as a means for achieving immediate goals—the abolition of the fetters of war economy. When it became necessary to find a proper representation of the Schleswig-Holstein farmers in the national and Prussian constitutional assemblies, they thus formed the *Schleswig-Holsteinische Bauern-und Landarbeiter-demokratie,* later called *Schleswig-Holsteinische Landespartei.* This was done with the tactically sound idea of supplementing the special interest organization (which pursued merely the rather narrow economic interests of the farmers) by a

---

[42] The *Bauernverein* had 35,000 members in 1923.
[43] Ermland is the only Catholic part of eastern Prussia.

political organization, which in the coming campaigns could win votes outside the farmer class, especially in the small town middle classes by incorporating political planks favored by them in the new party's platform. The co-operation of teachers, ministers, petty officials, and other non-farm elements, the formulation of a complete program, touching upon all fundamental questions of political life, would have enabled the new party to attain an importance similar to its namesake, the *Landespartei* of 1864, which in 1867 succeeded in occupying almost all seats in the *Norddeutsche Reichstag*. However, the successes of the *Schleswig-Holsteinische Bauern-und Landarbeiter-demokratie* remained limited to those sections where the *Bauernverein* had gained ground; whereas, in 1919 it received in the whole of Schleswig-Holstein on the average 7.2 per cent of the votes (in the country about 15 per cent, while almost none in urban districts). It was the strongest party in Landkreis Flensburg (45 per cent); second strongest (after the Social Democrats) in Kreis Rendsburg (27.5 per cent); of considerable importance in Schleswig, Bordesholm, Segeberg, and, at the North Sea coast in Husum, Dithmarschen, Eiderstedt; and weakest in South Tondern. Only in 1919 did the party win a seat in the Reichstag.

After a disastrous defeat in the elections of 1921 the *Landespartei* did not recover. The probable reasons for its downfall were these: lack of political experience among those strata of the middle classes from which it was recruited, the suspicion of separatistic leanings aroused by the activities of some of its supporters in the nobility and in the urban upper classes, and lack of affiliation with one of the great national parties.

In the campaign of 1924, the *Bauernverein* changed

its political tactics and looked for "parliamentary cross-connections." It succeeded in having one of its candidates nominated and elected by the *Deutschnationale Volks-partei,* one by *Deutsche Volkspartei,* and one by the *De-mokratische Partei.*

Though the *Landespartei* remained insignificant as a political force, it nevertheless is extremely interesting sociologically and historically. The history and structure of this party presents the inception of certain material and ideological factors to which National Socialism owed its, success in Schleswig-Holstein.

The *Schleswig-Holsteinische Landespartei* presents a rare opportunity to study a historically important movement, the National Socialist movement, at one of its origins. Instead of tracing the connections between Hitler's "philosophy" and those of Nietzsche, Houston Stewart Chamberlain, Fichte, and the Racists of the nineteenth century, we can here observe the inception of ideas, which later were transformed into the National Socialist party doctrine, by the anonymous masses of rural people who are not likely to give expression in writing to their ideas and beliefs. By analyzing the *Landespartei* ideology we can carry the analysis of the development of the National Socialist doctrine to a societal level which is not easily accessible to the student of the history of political ideas. Nazism, like democracy, begins at the "grass roots" and here we are able to pull some of these "roots" for close inspection. Furthermore, the *Landespartei* was not a singular and isolated phenomenon. It was in touch with similar movements for the establishment of regional autonomy in other regions which had been annexed by Prussia in 1866, such as the *Hessische Volksbund* and the *Welfen* party in Hannover, and also with the Bavarian particularists. Representing these centrifugal tendencies, the *Landespartei* can be regarded as a typical phenomenon of the immediate postwar years.

At first glance the *Landespartei* seemed to be a liberal party because of its relation to the *Bauernverein* which stood for economic laissez faire. This impression was strengthened by the fact that some of its leaders were trying to establish alliance with liberal politicians and parties in the parliaments of Prussia and the Reich. A more thorough examination of its ideology shows, however, that it by no means represents a purely liberal but rather a partly conservative, partly romantic conception of state and society. The pronounced emphasis on states' rights, the demand for administrative and cultural autonomy for Schleswig-Holstein within Germany, the demand for a second house of the legislature based upon industrial representation, the anti-Semitism which soon became apparent,[44] but foremost, its fundamental political concepts of the state and of the economic system—these are the points which distinguished this party from liberalism. If the members of the *Landespartei* formerly called themselves liberals, they did so because they wanted to be regarded as the successors and trustees of traditional Schleswig-Holstein liberalism. They emphasized that they were not to be identified with the new national *Demokratische Partei* and declared: "We of the *Landespartei* claim to be the representatives of the old Schleswig-Holstein liberalism. Democracy as conceived in Schleswig-Holstein is something entirely different from democracy as for instance represented by the *Berliner Tageblatt* or the *Frankfurter Zeitung*. The Schleswig-Holstein democracy . . . is a

[44] Cf. *Program of the Landespartei* (Kiel, no date), p. 9, "Any predominance of the Jews in business and government we shall fight with all our energy."

green democracy in contrast to the golden democracy." [45]
Demands like "freedom in economic life" and criticism
of economic postwar regulations, which were in accordance
with the program of the *Bauernverein*, were combined
with economic ideas, which were not any longer in accord
with liberalism. "The craftsman," according to the party
program, "has to be protected on the one hand against
capitalism, which crushes him by means of its factories,
and on the other hand against socialism, which aims at
making him a proletarian wage-laborer. At the same time
the merchant has to be protected against capitalism in the
form of the great department stores, and the whole retail
trade against the danger of socialism." The program continued: "By cautiously controlling big business, the spirit
of free enterprise and competition are not to be suppressed,
but the dangers involved in large capitalistic enterprise
should be diminished for the independent small craftsmen
and traders." Finally, it stated: "We demand that capital
and business submit to national interests." Thus the program established the primacy of politics.

While the similarity of these theses to certain points
in the program of the Nazis is striking, it should be noted
that they reiterated merely the old credo of reactionary

---

[45] Speech by the farmer Iversen-Munckbrarup at Rendsburg, Jan. 1,
1921, quoted from *Der Schleswig-Holsteiner* (Jan. 8, 1921). "Green"
and "gold" stand respectively as symbols of a national, agrarian-rooted
society and an international commercial cosmopolitan society. Considerable
difficulty is experienced in translating quotations from the party propaganda literature because of the lack of clarity characteristic of the language of the National Socialist movement and some of its precursors.
This is, of course, in itself a sociologically significant phenomenon. For
the nebulous character of the language of these political movements is due
partly to their "romantic" roots, partly a device—though by no means
always consciously and intentionally applied—to appeal to sentiments and
emotions rather than to clear thought; the ambiguity of these expressions
fitted well into a situation in which an appeal had to be made to a public
of great diversity in class position and interests.

Mittelstands-politik. Considering the origin of the party, it is not surprising that the farmers should be regarded as the very foundation (*der erste Stand*) of national economy. This in itself does not betray any anti-liberal attitude. The party program, however, contains certain ideas about the social functions of the farmer class which may help to explain the later anti-liberal about-face of many of its members.

"For the farmer," we read in the program, "living and working are the same." All conditions should be removed which might distort the old exemplary farmer's spirit, "the spirit concerned with the work rather than with the return from it." Thus the liberal economic concept of the "progressive farmer," which does not acknowledge any difference between the industrial or commercial entrepreneur's function and the farmer's work, is rejected. Here, already, the later National Socialist ideal of detaching the farmer from the capitalistic market economy becomes visible. Undoubtedly this ideal did agree, not so much with the economic purposes of the *Bauernverein* as with the ideology of some intellectuals in the *Landespartei*.

The federalism,[46] to which the party owed its existence, did not originate in the liberal tradition. Liberal thinking presupposes (even if, for tactical reasons, it associates with federalism) the affirmation, in principle, of the modern state with its centralized bureaucratic administration, and with its tendency towards uniformity and national integration. It was, however, precisely this type of state which the leaders in the *Landespartei* rejected. They regarded it as incongruous and dangerous to the Schleswig-Holstein spirit. The Prussian state was looked upon by the

---

[46] *Foederalismus* in German stands for a mere confederation of states instead of a centralized Reich. The term thus has the opposite meaning of the American term *federalism*.

intellectual leaders of the *Landespartei* as the incarnation of industrialism.

Thus the farmers' aversion to the policy of war economy was but a symptom of a deeply ingrained attitude which had been taken over from the older generation. This attitude originated from the country's actual political structure in pre-Prussian times. The "weak state," at which they were aiming, was not identical with the state of liberalism, which is supposed to be based upon an atomistic society, but was rather conceived of as a political corporation organically composed of naturally grown communities: villages, towns, and estates (*Stände*). The repudiation of the Prussian system was maintained chiefly by pointing out that the mistakes of the Prussian political system had caused the defeat in the last war and especially the loss of North Schleswig (a loss which at this time had not yet taken place but was expected). Prussia had never recognized Schleswig-Holstein's role of being the link between the Germanic South and the Germanic North. Therefore, the *Landespartei* regarded the *Deutschnationale Volkspartei* as its most severe adversary among the non-socialist parties. To them they were the representatives of Prussian conservatism, the men in charge of Prussian-German politics up to the time of the collapse. The criticism of Prussian policy in North Schleswig, the demand for native civil servants, the refusal to accept Berlin as the general center of culture were all outlets for a disposition which had been formed a long time before the war and had prevailed even from pre-Prussian times.

At bottom, the criticism against Prussia was merely an expression of a general antipathy against the social system of industrial capitalism, originating in a rural-conservative attitude, a criticism of *Gesellschaft* (society) out of a spirit of *Gemeinschaft* (community). The Prussian era, which had brought the great economic uplift for Schleswig-Holstein, was identified with the age of commercialization and industrialization, with the breakdown of good taste and the suffocation of creative cultural and administrative activity in the province. This anti-Prussian attitude distinguished the *Landespartei* from the conservative "young-nationalism" to which they were related in their criticism of the state and in their emphasis on the folk-idea.

The same philosophical point of view was also used in order to justify the very existence of the *Landespartei*. The Schleswig-Holstein man, with his "soul," could not fit entirely into any other party. This is the theme which Iversen elaborates in an editorial in the first issue of the *Schleswig-Holsteiner*.[47] All other parties had appealed only to the rational mind. "The Schleswig-Holstein man, however, wants to belong to a party which offers something for his soul as well." He especially expected the politicians to take consideration of the "tribal," i. e., regional, characteristics of the people, just as he demanded this from the civil servants. That is why the Low German dialect was used in the campaign whenever possible. These utterances are symptomatic of the state of mind prevailing in leading circles of the *Landespartei*. They entitle us to align the *Landespartei* with the wide-spread longing for "community" which, after the war, had seized the more intellectual circles of the middle classes. The party's attitude towards the state also becomes understandable on these premises. Lastly, the anti-Prussian federalism originated in a deep dislike of the modern state itself. The modern state was looked upon as the Leviathan, which devours all organically grown associations, decomposes all organic order, and dissolves all regional originality of political life. This attitude was certainly an anachronism.

[47] Cf. the issue of July 2, 1920.

It becomes understandable, however, if one realizes that until the middle of the nineteenth century true remnants of medieval political order were still alive in Schleswig-Holstein, i. e., the manifold nature of law and administration and the especially far-reaching nature of self-government of the rural farm village community—conditions which had to give way to Prussia's attempts to unify and bureaucratize the province. This animosity against the modern state appears to be less remote from reality if one considers that the oldest people among the living remembered the time when, for instance, the farmers of Eiderstedt themselves exercised the administration and jurisdiction of their territory.

On the other hand the political ideology of the *Landespartei* contained one conception which was to be spread during the following years by the ethnic movement and which was to be declared the principle of the Germanic theory of the state by the National Socialist party: to master the societal, institutionalized character of the modern state by rooting it in the ethnic community. The relationship with National Socialism is quite obvious when one analyzes the antithesis, in *Landespartei* language, of the people (*Volk*) and the State as *gemeinschaftliche* (community like) and *gesellschaftliche* (societal) principles. Likewise, the fostering of community spirit as a means of achieving the classless state and the longing for the "leader," which occasionally could be heard in the press of the *Landespartei,* point towards elements in their ideology which are related to National Socialism.[48]

The most important contrast, however, to the later National Socialism is the "quietistic" state of mind which had

[48] Cf. "Unsere Politische Not" in *Der Schleswig-Holsteiner* (Jan. 15, 1921), by Dr. Johs. Feddersen, who became one of the first members of the NSDAP in Schleswig-Holstein.

also been responsible for the tactics of the *Landespartei;* we understand by this term an attitude found in pietistic circles and sects, transferred to politics.[49] Connections of the leaders with pietistic circles can be traced in several cases, and pietist influence becomes quite obvious in the language of the *Landespartei* publications. A renewed and heightened consciousness of the ethical values of the folk and concentration on the "inner life" are the means by which the *Landespartei* expected a political regeneration. If Hedemann-Heespen[50] set his hopes in "forces having remained in the dark for centuries," in "the mute party," and especially in the rural middle classes, also in the "quiet ones in the country," this seems significant as indicative of the state of mind in wide circles of the *Landespartei.* Simplicity and quietness, these two elements of rusticity, appear to Hedemann as the foundation of community, as a counterpoise to a "rootless individualism." He saw the value of the *Landespartei* in its endeavor to realize the ideal of an organic corporate (*staendisch*) state on a rural foundation.

This same ideology is to be found in the *Hessische Volksbund,* which stood in connection with the *Landespartei.* Thus in its program we read: "Such a blossoming [of the fatherland] we do not find in the accomplishment of external power and of ideas hostile to peace, but in a real rejuvenation of the inner life and action through contemplation." Another proclamation from federalist cir-

---

[49] For this idea the author is indebted to Dr. Hans Gerth, who analyzed the sources pertaining to the *Landespartei.*

[50] Paul von Hedemann-Heespen, of Deutsch-Nienhof near Kiel, author of *Schleswig-Holstein und die Neuzeit* (Kiel, 1926), was one of the last true conservatives in Schleswig-Holstein. He represented the Schleswig-Holstein equivalent of that type of Southern planter philosophy which finds expression in William Percy's *Lanterns on the Levee.* The quotations are from the introduction to the volume cited.

cles runs: "Only a return to the inwardness (*Innerlich-keit*), which is a typical German characteristic, can save us. It is the basis of federalist thinking and the German state should be founded on it." [51] The anti-imperialist renunciation of material power and greatness of the state also becomes understandable through this political quietism. After the enormous consumption of physical and nervous strength and energy during the war, after years of intense submission of the individual in the service of the state, such an attitude could not but find susceptible minds among the farmers and the middle classes. Occasionally there can be found in the *Landespartei*'s publications the picture of a unified Europe built up from states federalistically organized on a regional (*Stammes*) basis.[52] This philosophical reasoning was not disinterested, however. The decentralized state appeared to the federalists to guarantee the political power of the middle classes, while in a centralized state, big business would always rule.[53]

Obviously this kind of federalism proved to be an anach-

[51] "Mahnung zur Einigkeit" by the secretary of the *Deutsch-Hannover-schen Partei*, in *Ruf zur Sammlung an alle deutschen Foederalisten*, No. 1 (July, 1921).

[52] "We federalists don't want politics comparable to the power politics of the European states before the war. Instead, we want a federalist union of Europe aiming at something similar to what the United States of America have achieved: the United States of Europe. This would be the only way to overcome the disease of the last century: nationalism," thus wrote E. Landweger (pseudonym of one of the younger intellectuals in the *Landespartei*) in 1922 in a pamphlet entitled: "Why is it that Everybody in Schleswig-Holstein Ought to Vote for the *Landespartei?*"

[53] An anonymous contribution to the federalist periodical, *Ruf zur Sammlung*, contains the following argument: "Big business will always favor centralization for the simple reason that, after establishing control of the central government, it can promote its interests in the whole country and indeed the better the more tensely, the more uniformly the central administration is organized."

ronism and quite inadequate as a solution to middle class problems, particularly so when in the course of the inflation a new, impoverished semi-proletarian middle class came into existence. This class had to look for the kind of social policy which presupposes a strong central government. This class also was dependent on the prosperity of "big business" rather than on the small artisan or merchant.

The *Landespartei* has historical importance because it helped to paralyze the "red wave" and also because it helped to prepare the ideological dispositions on which Nazism later could grow. Perhaps without this preparation the transition to National Socialism would not have occurred as quickly as it actually did in Schleswig-Holstein, especially on the *Geest,* that is, precisely in the sections of former influence of the *Landespartei.* It is further important that some of the leading National Socialists began their political career in the *Landespartei.*

Another social movement which has contributed to turning the farmers away from liberalism is the Young Farmer's Movement (*Jungbauern Bewegung*). Originally it was planned to be the youth organization of the *Bauernverein* and therefore held close contact with the *Landespartei.* Its origin was in Angeln where broad circles of the farm youth had already been activated politically in defense against Danish propaganda during the time of the plebiscite. In 1922, the year after the loss of North Schleswig, on the day of the battle of Leipzig, the first *Jungbauernschaft* was founded in the village of Schaalby, Angeln. Its founder was one of the leading men in the *Bauernverein,* who later became a champion of National Socialism. Starting in Angeln, the Young Farmers' Movement spread especially in the *Kreise* of Flensburg, Schleswig, Süd-Tondern, Eckernfoerde, and Rendsburg. It has never been a mass movement and could not have been because of its character. Its influence on the formation of political volition thus cannot be regarded as important, but the mere fact that such a movement could develop and prevail for many years, that a periodical was edited, that meetings and training courses were organized, and that considerable influence on youth in several villages was gained, is significant as a symptom of the unrest among Schleswig-Holstein country people.

Connections with the youth movement are evident. They were formed in the cultural struggle for North Schleswig, in which the *Wandervogel* and other youth organizations participated actively. The program of the Schleswig Association of *Jungbauernschaften* emphasizes this: "The *Jungbauernschaft* is a new youth movement." Gradually the concept "young farmer" was broadened, understood more symbolically, in such a way that not only the future farmers but all rural youths were permitted to join. The National Socialist idea of bridging differences of state and class by cultural meetings and common parties thus can be observed here.

The aim of the *Jungbauernschaften* can be briefly described as the forming of an economically efficient, politically trained farmers' elite of firm character. The necessity of rational technique and business methods on the farm was admitted, but they were to be applied in a peasant spirit, i. e., the farmer was not to become an entrepreneur to whom his farm was nothing but an investment. They were to find a synthesis between the tradition-bound farmer, living in "community," and the rational businesslike farmer.

The practical work of the *Jungbauernschaften* was done by study groups which embraced one or more villages, frequently under the leadership of a teacher who had formerly been a member of the youth movement. These study groups often were supplementary to the work of the folk high schools.

Perhaps the most unique and most important effect of the *Jungbauernschaften* has been their revival of the sense for regional and rural culture and their cultivation of songs, games, and folk dances. It was work which quite intentionally was done quietly, without any propaganda, and which purposely held aloof from direct political activity. This attitude, which originated from the same sources as the political quietism of the *Landespartei,* later led the movement into a difficult position over against the National Socialist party, which was so decidedly aiming at success among the masses and at seizure of power. While, in the course of time, the *Jungbauern* approached ideologically Nazism, still they remained separate in certain principles. The *Jungbauernschaften,* according to their religious foundation, could not but negate the primacy of politics over things of the spirit. They further disliked the subordination under a party with the structure of a religious order under authoritarian leadership, since for their own movement co-operative activity was essential. In this respect they were related to the more "democratic" *Jungdeutsche Orden.*[54]

This organization likewise stood in opposition to the old conservatism, and therefore found its adherents in the country among the middle classes, in industrial, commercial, and intellectual circles of villages and small towns rather than among farmers. It did not attain as much importance in Schleswig-Holstein as in other sections of north Germany.

---

[54] The *Jungdeutsche Orden* can best be defined sociologically as a democratic movement based on an organic theory of state, vested in fascistic forms of organization.

Both movements, like other ethnic and semi-military *Bünde* which emerged during the postwar period, differed from National Socialism in their lack of determination to seize power. Few of these *Bünde* succeeded in gaining a permanent foothold. Only the *Werwolf*, that anti-Semitic offshoot of the Steel Helmets, gained considerable following, mostly in north Dithmarschen. Here, in February, 1926, the following *Bünde* joined: *Wiking* (Ehrhard adherents) *Werwolf*, and *Stahlhelm West Küste* (the latter Bund differing from the original Steel Helmets in its greater political radicalism and outspoken anti-Semitism). These circles again had close connections with the *Tannenbergbund*,[55] which for some time seems to have been a sort of confederation of radical ethnic associations. In Schleswig-Holstein it had its main following on the *Geest* of Holstein (there are said to have been in 1930 about 26 locals in Kreis Rendsburg alone). Political sectarians of varied kinds got together in the *Tannenbergbund*, frequently religious people who had come to a break with the church and found a semblance of new creed in the writings of Mathilde Ludendorff; their attitude towards the state was at bottom extremely liberal with a touch of anarchism. It is not merely incidental that there were certain personal connections between the *Tannenbergbund* and the *Landvolk* movement, to be discussed later.

To estimate how far the ethnic movement, and with it, National Socialism, was stimulated by the loss of North Schleswig is scarcely possible. The question is of fundamental importance as it is known that Germans from re-

---

[55] This was General Ludendorff's organization which had seceded from the Nazi movement after the break between Hitler and Ludendorff. See Sigmund Neumann, *Die deutschen Parteien. Wesen und Wandel nach dem Kriege* (Berlin, 1932). While Ludendorff acted as leader, the philosophy was the creation of his second wife, Mathilde Ludendorff, née von Kremnitz.

gions of nationality conflict have played an important role as National Socialist leaders. Various personnel connections existed between the *Bauernverein,* the *Landespartei,* the Young Farmers' Movement, and the most important agency in the nationality conflict, the *Schleswig-Holsteiner Bund.* The war generation held the leadership in the *Schleswig-Holsteiner Bund* as in other organizations of its kind. This association likewise is to be regarded as a root-bed for National Socialism. Its concept of the nationality struggle in North Schleswig as a primarily cultural problem, the denial of a stern territorial irredentism (for instance, of the formula: What had been German territory would have to become German again), the recognition of ethnic conditions as the basis for boundary adjustments—all these ideas agreed in principle with the proclaimed minorities policy of the National Socialist party.[56]

This attitude induced the hostility of the *Deutschnationale Volkspartei* in such a way that the landed aristocracy did not participate in its work but rather fought it, as they had opposed any moderate policy in the treatment of the Danish minority based on understanding of the complex ethnic situation in the border zone.

The great successes of the National Socialists after the re-establishment of the party thus were ideologically prepared by a variety of ethnic movements. These, it should be noted, drew their support mainly from the smaller farmers, from school teachers, agricultural technologists, and other groups of the middle and lower strata of the rural middle classes, or to use the most precise German term, from among the *Mittel-* and *Kleinbauern* and the *Kleinbuergertum* of the small towns. The upper strata of

[56] The true intentions of the leadership of the party, which have become apparent only since 1938, were not discernible to the rank and file in the ethnic movement at that time.

big farmers, the large landowners and the rural bourgeoisie remained rather unshaken in their political conservatism.

The relationship between the Conservatives and the
National Socialists was rather ambiguous. Many Conservatives in Schleswig-Holstein and elsewhere, while de-
spising the personnel of the Nazi party and disapproving
of certain features of Hitler's policy, nevertheless welcomed the entire "ethnic" movement as an instrument for
attaining their own purposes and as a kind of nationalistic
revival which finally would lead the masses of the "awak-
ened" back into the fold of the Conservative party. Consequently, relations among the *Deutschnationale Volkspartei,* other conservative organizations and the various
"ethnic" movements tended to be quite cordial, if not
openly so, at least behind the scenes.

The conservative forces were organized mainly into
three groups: the *Deutschnationale Volkspartei,* the
Landbund, and the *Stahlhelm* (Steel Helmets).

Of these organizations, the *Stahlhelm,* in its beginnings,
was least committed to the Conservative party standpoint.
As a *bund* of all World War veterans, restricted only by
the prerequisite of a certain amount of actual combat service, it had to leave undetermined its position on questions
of practical politics and even the new constitution of the
Reich. Many of the younger generation among the ex-
soldiers dreamed of overcoming the distinctions of social
status and class. They hoped the new organization would
perpetuate that fellowship of all classes which they had
experienced in the trenches. One of the earliest proclamations of this sentiment, the speech of the student Theodor
Bartram, at the inauguration of the *Bund deutscher Front-
soldaten an deutschen Hochschulen* (*Bund* of German
combat soldiers at German universities) at Kiel Univer-

sity, February 26, 1919, manifested obvious relations with
the ideologies of the youth movement and also of the
Landespartei.

The older generation in the Steel Helmets had scarcely
been touched by such notions, since they were still imbued
with the ideas of the Wilhelminic era, or even impressed
with an ideology which received its inspiration from the
symbolic, idealized figure of Frederick the Great. Since
offices in this military organization were bestowed largely
according to the military rank of the members, the younger
generation did not have much of a chance to gain influence.
The splitting off of the *Werwolf* was a result of this conflict between the generations. In Schleswig-Holstein the
Werwolf participated in the above-mentioned merger of
militant ethnic *Bünde,* which had competed in Dithmarschen since 1924 with the Steel Helmets proper under the
name of *Stahlhelm Westküste.*

The Steel Helmets, however, developed more and more
in the rural parts of Schleswig-Holstein into an organization which had its support mainly among the owners of
large estates and large farms with their adherents. This
became obvious during the short life of a conservative
government in the second half of 1932. Conceived originally as a movement to restore the community of the people by the example of the fellowship of veterans, the Steel
Helmets had lapsed into a political instrument of the upper classes.

During the first years after the war, the Conservative
party had been very weak in the rural parts of Schleswig-
Holstein. The reactionary Kapp *Putsch* of 1920 had been
a complete failure in this region, and as late as 1923 any
plans for a conservative *putsch* met with stubborn opposition among the farmers. Nevertheless, in the elections of
1921, the *Deutschnationale Volkspartei* was the second

party in voting strength in the rural areas, surpassed only by the Social Democratic party. The *Deutschnationale Volkspartei* was not a mere continuation of the old Conservative party. By winning over certain strata of the urban population, including elements of the so-called "new middle class," it had attained a broader field of potential influence than the old Conservatives had ever possessed. The DNVP had a fair chance of becoming a popular conservative party. As such, it would have been capable of winning over the former "national liberal" and "progressive" farmers, for they succeeded in 1924 in getting almost 50 per cent of the rural vote on the *Geest* and about 40 per cent in the marshes and in the East. This development was cut short when in October, 1928, Hugenberg and the large manufacturers' wing gained control of the DNVP.

Although the Conservatives soon had regained a fair amount of success in the elections, the political leadership of farmers was not any longer really in their hands since the *Bauernverein* had started to compete with the *Landbund* and in some areas had even replaced it. The existence of an independent organization of the Schleswig-Holstein farmers, which maintained contacts with democratic organizations in other parts of the Reich, was felt as a serious threat by the Conservatives. In these years, after the stabilization of the Reichsmark, the Dawes agreement, the German-Russian treaty, and the beginning of industrial recovery, the new democratic state seemed to get more firmly established. That respectable Schleswig-Holstein farmers should join the supporters of the new democracy meant for the east Elbian landowner class a severe loss of prestige regardless of the loss of votes. Besides, the *Bauernverein* decidedly represented the economic interests of the cattle raisers and cattle grazers, and could therefore easily be driven into opposition against those landowners whose position in price and tariff policy was that of grain and potato growers. The fight, which for this reason the *Landbund* and the *Deutschnationale Volkspartei* put up in Schleswig-Holstein against the *Bauernverein,* was thus only part of the general struggle between the economic associations of large landowners and the farmers' organizations.

The position of the Conservatives in this struggle was at first disadvantageous on account of the disintegration of the prewar *Bund der Landwirte* in consequence of the breakdown of the imperial regime. Even after its reorganization into the *Landbund* the Conservatives remained weak.

The *Bauernverein,* on the other hand, was able, in the elections of December, 1924, when the *Landespartei* had ceased to exist, to force the nomination of its own candidates on the tickets of the Democratic party, the *Deutsche Volkspartei* (DVP) and even the DNVP. This was achieved by a threat to nominate a separate *Bauernverein* ticket—a characteristic illustration of the strengthening of special interest organizations through proportional representation. Therefore, the Conservatives strove for control of the *Bauernverein.*

The first attempt to establish close collaboration between the *Landbund* and the *Bauernverein* was made late in the summer of 1924. The agreement lasted only for half a year. This episode led, however, to the founding of a separate association of small farmers and cottagers, the *Kleinbauern-und Kleinbesitzer-Verband der Westküste,* which had its main support in the marshes owing to the sharp class distinctions between large and small farmers. Even a new attempt to reach a lasting agreement between the provincial leaders of the two large organizations, an attempt which was made in 1927 with the good services of the *Regierungspraesident*,[57] failed because the *Land-bund* leaders refused to pledge adherence to the democratic regime and officially to sever connections with the DNVP.

Among the rank and file of the two organizations restiveness and antagonism against the democratic regime continued to mount, particularly when the price of hogs fell and credit difficulties increased. In some of the counties complete union of the two organizations had already been achieved. When it became apparent that negotiations between the provincial leadership of the two associations did not lead to any result, opposition leaders within both organizations called open-air mass meetings of farmers in all county seats. Owing to participation of the small town middle classes the total number of demonstrators amounted to about 140,000.

In the first place, these mass meetings were to draw attention to the threatened position of the agricultural debtor and, in addition, they were to force the merger of the farm organizations over the heads of the official leaders. The demands which were raised at these meetings concerned tariff, credit, and tax regulations, and ended with an appeal to all political parties to take care of a proper representation of agriculture on their tickets for the coming elections. It was further demanded that the three organizations representing farm interests immediately unite into one large organization which would represent a force not to be overlooked by anybody. This was one of the first proclamations of the idea of one big union of all farmers which later on found its realization in the National Socialist *Bauernschaft*. The platforms adopted at these

[57] An interesting example of the ways in which the Conservatives were able to enlist the support of the high bureaucracy even under a liberal regime.

meetings included the familiar cry of the *Landbund* for increased agricultural tariffs. The main concern was, however, with the matter of indebtedness and credit. It is easy to see why the clamors should have been loudest in the marshes and other areas of intensive, highly commercialized agriculture. Similar mass meetings were staged simultaneously in Ostfriesland, the coastal region between the Elbe and Ems rivers, where similar socio-economic conditions prevailed. These meetings, which were called by a small committee with no authority, hardly would have turned out so successfully had there not already been present since summer a deep dissatisfaction among the farmers with their organizations. Thus, they were ready for the slogan of a unified organization for all agriculture, from cottager to large landowner. That the placid, soberminded, and reserved Schleswig-Holstein farmers should have turned out in such masses for these open-air meetings and parades—thereby adopting a form of political conduct hitherto used only by labor organizations [58]—indicates how far the process of social fermentation had gone and how strong the opposition to the leaders in office had already become.

Henceforth, the merger movement proceeded along two lines: one, the *Landvolk* movement favored by the *Landbund;* the other one, the *Bauernbund,* split off from the *Bauernverein* in the summer of 1928, under the leadership of the two farmers Toennsen of Schaalby and Koehler of Buhnstorf, both sympathizers with National Socialism.

The new organization of the *Bauernbund* was the provincial association of the unions of *Landbund* groups with

---

[58] Dr. Alfred Vagts has been kind enough to inform me that similar mass meetings had been organized before the First World War by the *Bund der Landwirte* in the province of Hannover.

the *Bauernverein* groups which had sprung up in numerous counties. The *Landbund* leadership finally was compelled to merge its own reduced membership into this new organization which then assumed the name, *Schleswig-Holsteinischer Land-und Bauernbund*. This organization, in which the peasants numerically prevailed, was controlled, at first, by large landowners and their political friends among the large farmers. The attempt to absorb the remnants of the original *Bauernverein* failed because of the opposition of *Bauernverein* leaders both in Schleswig-Holstein and in the national association. The influence of the *Bauernverein*, however, waned in 1930 when the NSDAP declared a boycott against it. The way in which the *Landbund* attacked the *Bauernverein* corresponded exactly with the tactics it applied throughout the Reich against the independent farmers' organizations.

While the *Landbund* succeeded in breaking up the farmers' organization which supported the democratic regime, the Conservatives failed to achieve their real aim of bringing the peasantry into their political fold, because in the regions where the peasantry prevailed, the new *Bauernbund* was soon controlled by National Socialists. The failure of the Conservatives' ambitions was probably also caused by the fact that the *Landbund* leaders, while negotiating with the *Bauernverein*, encouraged those farmers' riots which shook the country after the fall of 1928. The unfortunate turn which these turmoils took must have discredited the *Landbund*.

The *Landvolk* movement originated in the summer and fall of 1928 when the farmers started refusing to pay taxes because of the increase in foreclosures. The dissatisfaction was used by a farmer in Eiderstedt, W. Hamkens, to arouse a militant opposition to the government among farmers, especially in the marshes. Thus this movement began in those areas which were most susceptible to depression. The new feature in this movement was the strict repudiation of participation in parliamentary government and the propagation of ":direct action"—refusal to pay taxes from the "substance," prevention of forced sales and of attachment of agricultural implements, boycott of farmers who did not collaborate, and refusal to co-operate with the present regime. The practical application of these tactics led to conflicts with the executive organs of the state, which resulted in mass sentences for the farmers involved, especially the two leaders, and produced unrest far beyond the region. Similar movements originated in Oldenburg, Saxonia, Thuringia, Pomerania, East Prussia, Hannover, and Silesia. In Schleswig-Holstein these incidents confirmed the opinion among the farmers that the present regime was the enemy of agriculture, that the farmer could not expect any protection from the democratic state but rather had to protect himself against it. The proud and lordly marsh farmers who were accustomed to think of themselves as the ruling class and to regard the gendarmes as the protectors of their rights and property were particularly angered when the armed state police were called out to disperse their own mass meetings and parades.

The *Landvolk* movement abstained from developing formal organization; they were apprehensive lest the will for action and the fighting spirit might dwindle under the influence of the bureaucracy that goes with an organization. Later on "emergency committees" were established to take care of the debtors' problems, and in these, depending on local conditions, *Landbund* leaders, Steel Helmets, or National Socialists participated. In some counties the emergency committees went so far as to demand refusal to pay contributions to the Chamber of Agriculture and other organizations and to invite the people to boycott the "vampire-like trusts, department stores, and consumers' co-operatives."

When finally a terrorist group sprang up in the *Landvolk* movement, which perpetrated "demonstrative" attacks on tax collectors' offices and courthouses, the more sensible farmers withdrew, and the National Socialist party also thought it advisable to keep aloof from the *Landvolk* movement; for, as the Gau-leader of Schleswig-Holstein pointed out in a circular, the party had been greatly impaired by having been associated with the *Landvolk* movement. After a serious riot in Neumünster, Adolf Hitler prohibited participation by party members in activities of the *Landvolk*.

It was unfortunate for the *Bauernverein* that it avoided taking any stand whatever when the first clashes between farmers and police occurred as the result of an order attaching cattle for the payment of delinquent taxes. The *Bauernbund*, however, had immediately declared its solidarity with the rioting farmers and demanded a series of economic measures of a distinct National Socialist character. Later, when the *Landvolk* movement fell into disrepute on account of bombings and the appearance of political adventurers as agitators, the *Bauernbund* as well took an official stand against it, without actually losing contact, however. On October 6, 1929, the *Land-und Bauernbund* published a program with an obvious trend towards National Socialism. Here the *Bauernbund* declared expressly that the Schleswig-Holstein farmer did not have any confidence in the "present regime of bureaucracy and party rule." At the same time it withdrew definitely from the *Landvolk* movement.

The *Landvolk* movement found its adherents chiefly in southern Holstein, in southern Dithmarschen, around the town of Itzehoe, and particularly in the interstitial zone between the marsh and the *Geest* and in the river marshes; on the Holstein *Geest* the village Hohn in Kreis Rendsburg was for some time a main stronghold of the movement. This pattern may be explained by the movement's dependence for support on the *Tannenbergbund* and the *Stahlhelm Westküste* and its affiliated organizations.

In order to understand the *Landvolk* movement, it is important to realize that its active circle consisted primarily of men who did not hold office either in the government or in the agricultural organizations. The official representatives of agricultural interests, however, from the chamber president to the magistrate and even to the leaders of the *Bauernverein* and *Landbund* were all connected with the democratic parliamentary state, and naturally were entangled in many ways with the political parties in power. The *Landvolk* people felt, with good reasons, that all these politicians would not be inclined to endorse more militant tactics of passive resistance. They themselves had scarcely anything to lose, at least not any political prestige, and were in this respect free to act.

The *Landvolk* movement presents a very interesting insight into the formation of political will within the rural population. It developed from a union of militant circles drawn from all conservative groups directed against the parties and the recognized agricultural associations. Personal connections existed with the *Deutschnationale Volkspartei*, the *Landbund*, the Steel Helmets, the *Werwolf*, the Pan-German Society, and the Ehrhard Circle, as well as with the *Tannenbergbund*, the *Deutschvölkische Freiheitsbewegung*, and the radical wing of the National Socialist party. The real nucleus of the movement was formed not only by professional revolutionaries, who may have had connections with "Organization C," [59] but also by some farmers, among whom Claus Heim was most outstanding. In relation to the National Socialist party, the *Landvolk* movement was at first a competitor. However, from the very beginning its chances were limited because its leaders had never aimed at seizing power, but rather saw their task in undermining the existing regime either by mere passive resistance or by intimidating state and communal officials (hence the bombings!). A rigid organization like the one which the National Socialists were building was precisely what *Landvolk* adherents rejected, partly out of fear of bureaucratic stagnation, partly because it was expected to be easier this way to escape suppression by the police. They also were making a virtue of necessity, since it was not likely anyway that broad masses of farmers would ever flock to this radical movement. The loose form permitted connections with various "rightist" associations, which in their turn would tolerate a "spontaneous" movement, whereas they would have fought as a competitor any real organization.

The ideology of the *Landvolk* movement was strongly National Socialist. When the movement broke down, the majority of its adherents went over to the National Socialists. With the breakdown of this debtors' rebellion, the poor chances for any separate action of farmers had been proved; it had not been able to win the favorable public opinion of the towns and of rural non-farmers. The National Socialist party on the other hand claimed to be a

[59] "Organization C" (for Consul) was a terroristic secret organization, stemming from those auxiliary units of the *Reichswehr* which were formed in the emergencies of 1919 and 1920. The Organization had been involved in the assassination of Erzberger and Rathenau and in several other political murders.

movement of the entire people. National Socialism could step in where the front against the "system" had been dilapidated on account of the breakdown of the *Landvolk* movement and the resulting weakening of the *Landbund* and of the Conservatives. In the country it spread mainly by means of the *Bauernbund* which soon displaced the *Bauernverein* everywhere.

Herewith a new platform for the economic contest had been created. The old type of representation of agricultural interests had lost out and the new attempt at spontaneous direct action also had failed. Thus the road was paved for the National Socialist party to capture the farm vote. This was proved by the elections of September 14, 1930.

Like all political movements in modern society, the National Socialist party in its beginnings was predominantly urban. The first local units were organized in Altona, Kiel, and Flensburg in the years 1924 and 1925.

In the rural areas of Schleswig-Holstein, the prospects for the party were at first bad; the form and content of Nazism seemed to be incompatible with the character of the people. Adolf Hitler, however, after a visit to some locals in Dithmarschen in the spring of 1929, observed that, although he had often been warned that National Socialism would never gain a foothold in Lower Saxony (Niedersachsen), he had always refused to believe it and had been right after all.

The rural organization of the National Socialist party gained its first stronghold on the Holstein *Geest* and spread much later to the eastern districts. One of the oldest and strongest centers was the little town of Albersdorf on the Ditmarsian *Geest*, situated on one of the main railroad lines. In 1929 there were about eighteen locals on the *Geest* of southern Dithmarschen while only five locals existed in the marshes. On the Schleswig *Geest* the party organization started to spread about a year later. Latest of all sections to be penetrated by the organization was the Schleswig hill zone.

The beginning of National Socialist propaganda among the Schleswig-Holstein farmers coincides approximately with the beginnings of the depression in agriculture. The *National Socialist Yearbook of 1927* (second edition) contains an article by the Gau-leader of Schleswig-Holstein, Hinrich Lohse,[60] "National Socialism and German Agriculture," which presents all of the essential points on which the agitation among rural voters was based.

The situation of German agriculture, Lohse said, was getting worse from year to year. International finance had put this last bastion of national independence under fire in order to break its resistance. The profitableness of agriculture was endangered since a "so-called German government" had signed unfavorable commercial treaties with some other states. The tariff of 1925 did not protect the interests of cattle breeders. The importation of frozen meat on the contrary was rather favored by such measures as the concession to an English firm to build a refrigeration plant in Altona. A Reichstag majority in favor of a protective tariff on meat could not be attained. Besides, the "international Jewish finance capital" was able to compensate such tariffs through its influence on freight rates. Back of it was the intention to destroy first the German meat production and then the cultivation of grain, for two

---

[60] Lohse was a native of a *Geest* village in Holstein, an ex-soldier who, after some adventures in business, became the main speaker for the *Landespartei* and later on one of the first organized members of the NSDAP in Schleswig-Holstein. As a man of lower middle class origin, of fragmentary education, and as a professional politician without a foothold in any other gainful occupation, he was quite typical of the "old guard" in the party.

reasons: to get a monopoly for foreign agriculture and to make the German people dependent for their food supply and thus force them to comply with the "Dawes servitude." The Marxian parties in rejecting agrarian tariffs for the benefit of the consumers made politics only for the day. The political leaders of agriculture, most of whom adhered to liberal capitalistic ideas, had not yet fully recognized the danger. Within the DNVP, the industrial group, which had close relations with the "international finance capital," had won complete control. The limitation of the party's activities to economic policy which had frequently been demanded by agricultural circles or even the foundation of a purely agrarian party was "nonsense, as long as parliamentary Germany was ruled by finance capitalism." Not pressure politics but only a strong "ethnic state" which would give the knockout blow to international finance capitalism would be able to aid agriculture.

Typically National Socialist is the idea that the agrarian interests alone as a minority would never have a chance under a democratic regime. This, of course, would be true only if the possibility of compromise were rejected. Such compromises actually had taken place in 1925 when the combined agrarian and industrial interests re-established a protective tariff system, very much against the advice of independent economic experts.

The tactical position of the National Socialist party in relation to the parties supporting the parliamentary democratic regime improved with the increasing depression. All parties responsible for the agricultural policy of the government were inclined to underestimate the effect and the duration of the depression and therefore tried to shape public opinion by optimistic statements. The National Socialists did the opposite. They demanded a fundamental change in the political system since only through an entirely new economic policy might the depression be overcome. For that reason they took an intransigent attitude in the provincial council (*Provinzial-Landtag*) into which seven representatives had been elected on November 17, 1929. "I shall tell you," the party leader from Eiderstedt, Otto Hamkens, a lawyer and farmer, addressed the administration parties: "Not only this year we have an emergency, but there will be more such years, and then you will be at the end of your wits. . . . The budget of the day leaves us quite cool. We don't enter the legislatures in order to collaborate positively. We can collaborate only with the aim of overthrowing the present system of government. Only then will we be able to do constructive work!" This uncompromising attitude gave the National Socialists a tactical advantage over their most dangerous opponent, the DNVP. The Conservatives had lost much of their popularity because of their wavering course in questions of foreign affairs and because of the split in the party when Hugenberg, who was regarded as the agent of heavy industry, took over the party leadership in the fall of 1928.[61]

The younger generation in particular seceded and joined the National Socialists either directly or at first by going over to groups of young Conservatives. Among these only the *Landvolk Partei* gained any importance in Schleswig-Holstein. The attempts of the *Landbund* to prevent farmers from voting for Hitler by lending support to the *Landvolk Partei* were, however, of little effect. Young Conservative circles among farmers as early as 1930 probably had sympathized more with the National Socialists than with the *Deutschnationale Volkspartei*, which was supported by large landowners and big capital, representing entrepreneur interests with only a slight touch of

61 Cf. Neumann, *op. cit.*, pp. 62 ff.

employees' influence through the German National Association of Commercial Employees (*Deutschnationaler Handlungsgehilfen Verband*). Hugenberg's leadership further antagonized these circles. The farmers' tradi-tional antipathy to Prussian conservatism was combined with the anti-capitalistic feeling of the "new middle class" in the neo-Prussian Schleswig-Holstein.

Thus it came about that the *Bauernbund* did not become the dutiful tool of conservative leaders of the *Landbund,* but rather an outpost of National Socialism in the rural areas. This becomes understandable if one considers that the 37,600 members of the *Bauernbund* were for the most part the same men who had been fighting against the Con-servatives since 1918—in the *Landespartei,* in the Demo-cratic party, in the *Volkspartei,* and also in the ethnic movement. This applies particularly to the leaders.

It was solely the opposition to parliamentary govern-ment which made these men inclined to a temporary al-liance with the *Landbund* and the Conservative party (DNVP). They thought that in a highly industrialized society the farmers never would get decisive influence in the government through a legislature in which they were confronted with the two great blocs of industrial workers and industrial and commercial entrepreneurs. Apparently, an alliance of the "family farmers" with the Labor party, such as was effected some years later in Sweden, was never contemplated.

In the spring of 1930, after the receding of the second *Landvolk* movement in Schleswig-Holstein and at a mo-ment when the confidence of the farmers in the old parties had been considerably shaken, the National Socialist party stepped forward with its new agrarian program. Its main point was the re-establishment of profits through reduc-tion of production costs (reduction of the rate of interest,

prices of fertilizer, and rates for electricity), through lowering of commercial profits, through protective tariffs,
through simplification and lowering of tax assessments for
agriculture, and through lowering of land prices (prohi-
bition of land purchases for speculative purposes was proposed to prevent a further boom in real estate prices).
The labor problem was to be solved by firmly establishing
the agricultural laborer in the farm community through
socially just contracts instead of by collective agreements
as adapted from industrial labor policy. This proposal was
designed to win the favor of farmers and landowners without antagonizing too much the agricultural laborers. To
gain the support of the latter, competition of foreign sea-
sonal workers was to be excluded, improvement of housing
conditions was promised, and opportunities for advance-
ment to ownership were to be provided through resettlement policies. On the other hand, the formula of a
"healthy balance of large estates, medium and small
farms" indicated that no radical policy of resettlement
was intended, a statement which was to soothe the large
landowners. The foremost promise, however, was that
agriculture would be regarded as the privileged class *(der
erste Stand)* in the National Socialist state. The farmers,
especially in areas of strongly developed market production, Eiderstedt and Dithmarschen, had certain appre-
hensions about the relationship of the individual and the
state in National Socialism. But they were convinced that
in any event the farmer would be such an important factor
in the National Socialist state that he would be able to
shape the state according to his wants. Farmers made their
decision in favor of National Socialism because the National Socialist party appeared to pursue their interests
with more determination than any other party and because
the party leadership in Schleswig-Holstein was placed in

the hands of men who either were farmers themselves or who had at least come from farm families. Since the autumn of 1928, the NSDAP had had a newspaper of its own, the *Schleswig-Holsteinische Tageszeitung,* and in the spring of 1930 they secured almost full support from the influential *Kieler Zeitung.*

The elections for the provincial council (Provincial *Landtag*) of November 17, 1929, revealed for the first time the strength and regional distribution of the National Socialists; they won seven mandates out of sixty-one, five of which came from districts along the west coast. In Northern and Southern Dithmarschen, the National Socialist candidates obtained more votes than any of the others. The small enclave belonging to the state of Oldenburg (*Landesteil Lübeck*) became a main stronghold of the NSDAP when it entered the state government of Oldenburg; the propaganda in eastern Holstein was carried on from there.

In July, 1931, the supreme party leadership took a very decisive step by asking their members to join the *Landbund,* i. e., the *Land-und Bauernbund* in Schleswig-Holstein, "this great organization" in which, according to Adolf Hitler, "absolutely valuable forces are at work, which might also co-operate in the Third Reich, if placed in the right position." Thus, the *Land-und Bauernbund* was declared eligible for alliance; but, on the other hand, the struggle for the commanding positions in the organization was opened after the lower positions already had been filled by party members.[62]

The farmers' inclination to embrace National Socialism

[62] A description of this struggle, as it took place in Hessen, is given in Schmahl-Seipel, *Entwicklung der völkischen Bewegung* (Giessen, 1933). A similar relationship was effected in December, 1931, between the NSDAP and the *Nordwest-deutsche Handwerker Bund;* this facilitated the penetration of the NSDAP into the trading villages and small towns.

probably was strengthened by the fact that the "Green Front" under the influence of owners of large estates in the eastern parts of the Reich had been supporting the foodstuff policy of Dr. Schiele, which was contrary to the interests of the Schleswig-Holstein meat producers. The medium and small farmers, who furnished the main support of the NSDAP, were especially hit by this measure. It was for this reason that the *Bauernverein* under the leadership of the former *Landespartei* member, Iwersen-Munkbrarup, withdrew from the national association of *Bauernvereine* which was connected with the "Green Front." This step had caused further splits in the *Bauernverein*. At this moment the Nazi-controlled *Bauernbund* claimed and obtained a monopoly for all offices of self-government and farm organizations in the province. At the election of officers in the Chamber of Agriculture of Schleswig-Holstein in October, 1931, thirty-one out of the thirty-five representatives were its delegates.

The same technique of undermining was applied to the organizations of small manufacturers and businessmen, the industrial and commercial middle classes. The overwhelming success in the Reichstag elections of the summer of 1932 was due largely to this method of obtaining control of economic interest organizations.

In the fall of 1931 the great bank crash, increased difficulties in getting credit, and falling agricultural prices led to a new wave of direct action which took the form of tax strikes, strikes against paying interest, and prevention of forced sales of land. This movement became so threatening that the *Bauernbund* and the NSDAP decided to intercept it. The county units of the *Bauernbund* (*Kreis Bauernbunde*) themselves established self-help organizations. The *Bauernbund* initiated about a thousand meetings all over the province on October 10, 1931. The participants formed village associations (*Schicksalsge-meinschaften*) for the prevention of forced sales; they also were to strive for a moratorium. These groups did not stop at mere proclamations. Toward the end of October a rioting crowd of about a thousand farmers interfered by threats and intimidation with the forced sale of a *Geest* farm in the Kreis Steinburg. The *Deutsche Allgemeine Zeitung,* the important Conservative newspaper, thought it remarkable that this time the leaders seemed to be more temperate men and men of more importance than the participants in former *Landvolk* riots; the bitterness shown even by sober people who were perfectly willing to do their duty as loyal citizens seemed to indicate that this problem deserved more careful attention. Finally in November, 1931, a "Farmers' Co-operative for the Protection of Property" (*Landwirtschaftliche Besitz-schutzgenossenschaft e.G.m.b.H.*) with its headquarters in Kiel was founded in connection with the Schleswig-Holstein *Land-und Bauernbund.*[63] It endeavored to bring about settlements between farmers and their creditors and later helped to execute the debt-reduction plan of Mr. Hugenberg. Thus a movement, which had flared up in the country again and again for four years, was on the way to becoming "legalized" and centralized.

The proclamations and petitions which were decided upon in the meetings of October 10 convey a good insight into the sentiments of the peasantry and their demands. "Never before has the situation of agriculture on the west coast been so serious as today," ran the declaration of the *Kreis Bauernbund* of Southern Dithmarschen. "Formerly the inefficient and careless farmers went into bankruptcy; today also those farmers, and in even larger numbers, go

[63] At the time of its liquidation, May, 1934, this organization had approximately 3,100 members.

bankrupt who are diligent, who work efficiently and live modestly, who commit only the one mistake of actually trusting that the good advice we get from armchairs and green tables of the administration will help us to get ahead. We were fooled by accounts made up about intensifying, rationalizing, increasing production, and improving quality. Our farms have dropped to about half the value they had last year because of the low prices of agricultural products and the increased burden of interests. Fifty per cent of the farmers have had to declare their insolvency. . . . Dairying, stock fattening, raising of pigs and calves, truck farming—no branch of agriculture is profitable to-day. . . . The octopus arms of international finance capitalism are extended to us through all banks and savings banks." Therefore, they had met in order to bring about unification of all forces "that on the ruins of a bankrupt system a new Reich of youthful strength would arise, in which honest and diligent work would receive more justice than nowadays. . . . Long enough we have dissipated our forces because we used to think of ourselves too much as kings on our farms. . . . We cannot afford anymore to live in unconcern over the fate of our neighbor. That way we will go to the dogs one after the other." That is why 65,000 farmers had united in an emergency association, the aim of which was the prevention of forced sales by measures which would remove the causes. They demanded a sharp reduction of interest rates, measures against the importation of any kind of food which was produced in sufficient quantities in Germany, abolition of the unsound margin of merchants' profits, a lowering of all social, public, and other excessive burdens, i. e., taxes and contributions to social security, so as to adjust them to the farmers' ability to pay, abolition of the intolerable foreign debt and a sufficiently large government credit to finance a moratorium until agricultural prosperity was restored.[64]

The problem of indebtedness now was obviously in the foreground of people's minds. Psychologically revealing and important to the understanding of political developments is the renunciation of the marsh farmer's traditional individualistic attitude of being "king on one's farm." Significant, too, was the bitter disappointment about the failure of progressive capitalistic methods of management which were recommended and propagated by the official and co-operative institutions of German agriculture immediately after the war at a time of shortages in all commodities. These were indeed symptoms of a thorough change in mode of thought; economic liberalism had lost its meaning for these people. The "communities of fate" (*Schicksalsgemeinschaften*) devised their tactics accordingly. Only he who places himself in the common front will receive protection; he who does not do so is threatened with economic and social boycott as a traitor. It is proclaimed everybody's duty to act with solidarity in case of forced sales. But everyone who could pay his debts without hazard to his economic security was asked to comply with his obligations, in particular those to his own laborers and his fellow farmers.

Through all these channels—the *Bauernbund*, the *Schicksalsgemeinschaften*, the party organization proper, and the Brown Shirts—the National Socialist party succeeded during the years 1930 to 1932 in attracting the majority of the rural population, farmers and others. In the election of July 31, 1932, the NSDAP obtained 63.8 per cent of the rural vote.

In fact, in the summer of 1932, there were only three rural groups which still stood outside: the owners of large estates, or rather the older generation of them, since the

---

[64] *Schleswig-Holsteinischer Bauernbund*, No. 45 (Nov. 18, 1931).

younger ones had to a great extent already become National Socialists; the richest, and therefore, most respected large farmers; and finally, large parts of the agricultural working class, especially in areas of sharp class contrasts, where the Social Democratic party and the Communist party still had large followings.

In areas of less pronounced social differentiation the Marxist parties had not succeeded in retaining the rural workers, much less in extending the circle of their voters. In the country they had been on the defensive since 1924; their proportion of votes had decreased ever since 1919 (with the one exception of the election in 1928), although in the cities they were gaining from 1924 until the summer of 1932. The Social Democrats were, as a party of urban industrial workers, tactically in a very unfortunate situation when it came to canvassing rural areas. From their earlier more dogmatic past, the stigma of animosity towards the farmers was still attached to them. Since the Marxists set their hopes on an increasing concentration of capital or rather the increase of the proletariat, their adversaries thought that a vigorous peasantry on its own soil would be a thorn in their flesh.

The foodstuff policy which they advocated seemed to justify such criticism. The party itself did not manage to overcome this hostile attitude among the farmers by advocating constructive ideas. Its representatives in the Schleswig-Holstein provincial council (Provincial *Landtag*) did not make a serious attempt to free themselves from the antitheses of city-country, consumers-producers, or to appeal to the farmers' own interests.

The Communists, however, tried, by pointing out the differences of interest within the agricultural population, to win over not only the laborers but also settlers, peasants, cottagers, and fishermen, and to "neutralize" the

medium and small farmers. Following the tactical instruc-
tions of the action program of 1927, the Communists
pointed out the contrast between the industrial boom of
1927–1928 and the suffering of the agricultural and middle classes. "The year of 1927 was a year of prosperity
and this year may be called 'dictatorship of the national
industrial and commercial organizations' on the one hand,
and on the other hand 'the distress of agriculture.' " They
tried to play up the interests of dairying and meat production against those of grain cultivation and industry. They
opposed any tariff on feeds which would hurt the small
farmer in Schleswig-Holstein. For this reason they criti-
cized, in the campaign of 1931, the policy of moving the
hog-fattening industry to the eastern grain and potato
producing parts of Germany.

Since they did not bear any responsibility, they could
raise purely demagogic demands, like that for the can-
cellation of all taxes due from 1924 to 1926. The Communist farmer organizations which won some ground in
1931 and 1932 in Hannover and Ost Friesland seem to
have found no following of any importance in Schleswig-
Holstein, at least not among farmers.

In 1931 or 1932 there was founded under the leadership
of the former *Landvolk* editor, B. von Salomon, on the
Geest south of Itzehoe a Communist farmers' and workers' committee of action (*Bauern-und Arbeiter-Aktions-
komitee*) which tried to take the wind from the sails of
the National Socialist village associations (*Schicksalsge-
meinschaften*).

The Communists' schemes to unite small and medium
farmers with agricultural and industrial labor in a common front against large landowners and big business
met with particularly unfavorable prospects in Schleswig-
Holstein. On the one hand there was no broad class of

impoverished farmers cherishing the sentiment of being exploited and oppressed which, according to the Communists' own assumptions, would have been the precondition. Among the agricultural laborers on the other hand, communistic ideas were not likely to gain much sympathy because this class was in general too stable and too well connected to the land by ownership or other tenure of a house and vegetable patch or even, like the cottagers (*Insten*), by a share in the farm land.

The *Landarbeiter Verband,* a farm laborers' union affiliated with the social democratic *Freie Gewerkschaften,* which represented their demands for improved working conditions, stood in sharp opposition to the Communist party and did not hesitate to expel entire locals in which the Communists had obtained control (e. g., the local in Wesselburen in Dithmarschen). The only rural areas in which the Communists succeeded in inducing large numbers of farm laborers to join their party were those where sharp differences in wealth and tenure restricted the chances of climbing upwards on the ladder of tenure. These were chiefly the Isle of Fehmarn, the districts of large estates in eastern Holstein, and some of the larger villages in the marshes. Communist locals of importance sprang up also in some villages in the hinterland of the metropolitan center of Hamburg—perhaps in consequence of settlement of urban workers. Although the Social Democrats, even after the end of the inflation (1923), obtained more than one fourth of the rural vote in some elections, the Communists obtained only small percentages.

In the summer of 1932, therefore, neither the Marxist parties nor the old middle class parties had a strong following among the rank and file of the rural population. Then came the suspension of the democratic government of Prussia by a conservative Reich government. Although in the subsequent elections this led to slight increases in the Conservative vote, these were more than offset by the overwhelming victory gained at the polls by the National Socialists. The latter obtained over two thirds of the rural vote, the DNVP only 9.2 per cent, the two socialist parties (SPD and KPD) together not quite 25 per cent even though they won almost 45 per cent of the urban vote.

The successful appeal of the Nazis to the masses was not due merely to their opposition to the democratic regime—in this the DNVP had not lagged behind since Hugenberg had become the leader of the party. The Nazis' demands concerning economic policy were advanced also by other parties. The interests of the small farmers as opposed to big business were represented in the *Landvolk Partei,* in the *Christlich Sozialer Volksdienst,* and in the *Wirtschafts Partei.* None of these parties had been capable of winning such strong support of the masses as the National Socialists.

The peculiar mass appeal of this party probably was due to a large extent to the fact that the Nazis created not merely another party but an entirely new type of political machine which constituted a totalitarian movement in a double sense: first, in that it aimed at a monopoly of political power; second, in that it was not merely a fee-collecting organization but claimed the "entire man," demanding an exceedingly intensive participation in party work by its members. In this fashion, the movement offered a psychic outlet for the repressed ambitions and emotions of rural youth; it lent prestige and authority to persons of mediocre or subordinate positions in ordinary ways of life. The farmer's son whose ambitions for a career in the professions or in the army had been thwarted by the outcome of the war or by the economic vicissitudes of the postwar era, the man who instead of becoming a well-established lawyer or physician had to be content with a small practice as a dentist or the humble position of a milk inspector, felt elated when he could march through the streets of the county seat at the head of a troop of Brown Shirts and break up a Communist meeting.

Although this involved a burden particularly heavy for farmers during the busy seasons, the movement offered a new experience of fellowship of a very tangible nature; it offered a substantial backing in political and economic emergencies; it prevented forced sales; it secured patronage for the craftsman or retail dealer who joined the party; and it aided those who on account of their political activities had lost jobs or positions. These considerations explain the curious fact that these traditionally liberal farmers of strongly developed capitalistic mentality turned in such large numbers to a party whose agricultural program was based on the idea of a "just price," was directed towards a stabilization of farm incomes, and therefore led inevitably to far-going restrictions on the freedom of farm management. The drift towards National Socialism was perhaps largely conditioned by the excessive uncertainty of the markets for agricultural products in the postwar years. This insecurity had been felt with particular intensity in Schleswig-Holstein where most farms, and especially those with one-sided specialization, were highly dependent on the market. It is not difficult to understand that the smaller farmers, who are less given to speculative exploitation of marketing conditions than the large farmers and the operators of large estates, were anxious about the economic security of their families even at the price of their economic and personal liberty. The idea of security which appeared in 1919 as a mere ideology in the *Landespartei* had in the meantime become a widely accepted element of the farmers' class consciousness.

Furthermore, the importance of the belief in the "leader" should not be underestimated. Many farmers, when they felt at the end of their wits and when neither the government nor any of the other opposition parties seemed to be able to solve their problems, gave their vote not so much to the Nazi party as to Adolf Hitler. "He was our last hope," they would say afterwards; "we thought we might at last try it with him." Among the more zealous Nazis, of course, Hitler was regarded as a savior and liberator from all the troubles of the day. It is often said, however, that in rural Schleswig-Holstein the irrational elements of National Socialist thought had exerted scarcely any influence. The farmers, who are notoriously rather sober, calculating men, had voted the NSDAP ticket because they expected a Nazi government would rid them of their debts either by a moratorium or by inflation. According to our own inquiries, these motivations, although certainly of importance, seem to have been greatly overestimated at the time. Most people arrive at political decisions not by such purposive, rational deliberations but under the influence of tradition or from faith in the personality of outstanding leaders.

The other factors which contributed very considerably to the success of the NSDAP were its appeal to the younger generation and the chances which it offered to strata of rural society hitherto excluded from political leadership.

The NSDAP was, apart from the KPD, the only party

in which young men could hope to wield any influence or play a leading role. No wonder that even in the nobility the younger generation often joined the NSDAP. All other parties were directed by men past forty. Furthermore, as in most established, rather stable rural societies, political leadership in rural Schleswig-Holstein had been firmly in the hands of the owners of estates and large farms and their retinue among the professions. Now the NSDAP opened a new avenue of political ascent to the small farmer, the small businessman, the semi-professional classes of agricultural technicians, and even to those who never had established themselves successfully in any occupation. For, since the entire stratum of rural notables was more or less discredited on account of collaboration by its members with the democratic system as village magistrates, as officials of the Chamber of Agriculture, and in other agencies, a revolution against this regime inevitably led to the emergence of an entirely new stratum of political leaders and representatives. Thus, the attempts to restore the political dominance of conservative landlords and large farmers were doomed to failure, for when the Nazis seized power in 1933, most political offices and other positions of authority in the rural areas were occupied by persons from the middle strata of rural society.

The membership in the NSDAP in Schleswig-Holstein did not exceed fifty or sixty thousand before the end of 1932.[65] Provided that the organized followers of Hitler were at that time the convinced National Socialists, there is thus little reason to assume that the broad masses who voted for the NSDAP were up to 1932 intensively

[65] Computed from police reports to the *Oberpraesident* of Schleswig-Holstein. Kiel (*Oberpraesidium*).

steeped in the specific Nazi creed, or that they had a clear conception of all the tenets of Nazi ideology. Their voting for Hitler was primarily motivated by more or less tangible expectations which the National Socialists had evoked—expectations principally of improvement in their economic conditions.

Our analysis, however, has shown that certain elements of thought akin to National Socialist ideology had attained rather wide dispersion even before the NSDAP consolidated all the more militant currents of the counter-revolutionary opposition to the democratic regime. These elements can be classified into two major groups: first, a line of thought which can be described as a neo-romantic conception of the social order, at its best postulating an ideal state based on the "community of the people" (*Volksgemeinschaft*). While this line of thought in certain circles bordered dangerously close on anti-Semitism, it was as such not incompatible with democratic principles. The very ambiguity of these ideas made them acceptable to voters not at all disposed to give up civil liberties. There was, as previously indicated, closely interwoven with these notions the longing for charismatic leadership—the daydream of a new iron chancellor, a political savior who would solve all the dilemmas of the situation. However, nowhere in this complex of thought was there any anticipation of the complete abolition of the rule-of-law.

The inception of this most essential characteristic of the Third Reich is to be found in the second complex of elements of National Socialism. This was the line of thought which may be defined as "counter-revolutionary syndicalism." The resort to "self-help," to "direct action," the refusal to play the game of politics according to the rules of parliamentary democracy, the use of violence and intimidation against political adversaries [66] were the main features in this complex. They are essentially of revolutionary syndicalist vintage and were brought upon the political scene in Germany largely as imports from fascist Italy. Nothing proves more clearly the disintegration of middle class political ethics than the indulgence shown by broad circles of conservatives and even liberals in relation to the syndicalistic methods introduced into political life by the National Socialists and their forerunners. Blinded by their opportunistic view on political matters, the leaders of the farmers, businessmen, and even of the professional classes failed to visualize that the turbulent actions of the "Nazis" would finally lead to the destruction of the very foundation of the modern state, the rule-of-law, and result in tyranny.

[66] An analysis of election results by communities showed a rather strong inverse correlation between the size of the community and the percentage of votes obtained by the NSDAP. (Only the very small communities, mostly estates, did not correspond to this pattern.) This may be explained partly as a consequence of greater like-mindedness in small communities, partly, however, by the more effective social control and pressure exercised by the NSDAP once it had obtained a considerable support in such communities. There were, in 1931 and 1932, many rural communities where scarcely a barn door was not decorated with NSDAP posters. Anybody who knows the methods of social control applied by the Nazis will agree that such uniformity of behavior very likely was not entirely voluntary.

IV

THE ECOLOGY [67] OF POLITICAL PARTIES IN SCHLESWIG-HOLSTEIN

THE changing relations between the various political parties and the social classes in rural society which have been discussed in the preceding chapter can be more clearly demonstrated by a comparative analysis of election results in various subregions and in various types of communities.

Certainly in the political life of a modern nation, events in one region are more or less determined by events in other regions, and political processes tend to become nationwide rather than regional. Nevertheless, an intensive study of local variations in political processes, supported by a comprehensive knowledge of all relevant factors in the region, is likely to aid in a better understanding of political changes in the nation.

The student of political movements in pre-Nazi Germany was aided by the fact that a multiple party system lends itself better than a two party system to this kind of analysis. Furthermore, the system of proportional representation favored the organization of political parties

[67] The term "ecology" denotes the study of the distribution and constellations of social phenomena in space; that is, it refers to the observation and analysis of social facts in a given area or territory and in their co-existence and inter-relatedness. The term "sociography" which was invented by R. Steinmetz and adopted by Ferdinand Tönnies could very well be considered as an equivalent. (See R. Heberle, "Soziographie," *Handwoerterbuch der Soziologie* [Stuttgart, 1931].)

around definite social interest groups,[68] and therefore emphasized the correspondence between social classes and political parties. Consequently the party constellation in any area came very close to an expression of the class structure of the area.[69]

Schleswig-Holstein is particularly well suited for an ecological study because it comprises within a small area three distinct subregions which are also characteristic of north Germany in general. (See Figure 1.) The marshes along the North Sea coast, with their highly commercialized and specialized agriculture, extend towards the Dutch border; the sandy *Geest,* a family-farm region in the middle of the peninsula, has its continuation south of the Elbe River; and the eastern hill zone, with its large estates on loamy soils, is part of the Baltic hills which run through much of the north German plain east of the Elbe. Schleswig-Holstein thus combines the features of both western and eastern Germany in its structure of rural society.

No wonder, then, that the development of party con-

[68] The old system of Reichstag elections before 1918, with small election districts and majority elections, favored personality choices, brought the candidates into close contact with the constituents, and compelled those in the run-offs to compromise; the new system under the Constitution of Weimar with large election districts and proportional representation favored choices of an impersonal character: The candidates were unable to maintain close contacts with their constituents because the whole of Schleswig-Holstein was now one election district covering an area of 15,000 qkm., with a population of 1.5 millions, and each party presented a long list of candidates who had been nominated by party caucuses. The lower places on the list were usually filled with representatives of organized interest groups, often little known to the broader public.

[69] For the city of Hamburg, this has been shown by a series of maps prepared by Andreas Walther: "Die Oertliche Verteilung der Waehler grosser Parteien im Staedte-Komplex Hamburg auf Grund der Reichstagswahl, vom 14, September, 1930," *Aus Hamburgs Verwaltung und Wirtschaft, Monatsschrift des Statistischen Landesamts,* 8. Jahrgang, No. 6 (1931).

stellations in the elections to the Reichstag during the period from the First World War to the Nazi counterrevolution is also representative of the course of events in the Reich in general.

If the absolute numbers obtained by the main parties and combinations of parties in Schleswig-Holstein and in the Reich are compared (Figure 2), one finds the same constancy of the Marxist Socialist and Communist or Labor vote,[70] the same cyclical rise and fall of the Conservative vote; however, in Schleswig-Holstein the increase of the Nazi vote starts earlier, and the decline of the combined vote of the middle parties is much steeper.

The shrinking of the middle parties and the radicalization of the counter-revolutionary parties of the right is even more clearly demonstrated by the percentages of the total vote obtained by the major parties in Schleswig-Holstein (Table 3).

[70] The abbreviations and short designations used for political parties are as follows:

NSDAP: *Nationalsozialistische Deutsche Arbeiter Partei* (National Socialist German Labor Party) or "Nazis."

DNVP: *Deutschnationale Volkspartei* (German National Peoples Party) or "Conservatives."

DVP: *Deutsche Volkspartei* (German Peoples Party) or "Right Liberals."

DDP: *Deutsche Demokratische Partei* (German Democratic Party) or "Democrats"; this party later on changed its name to *Staatspartei.*

SPD: *Sozialdemokratische Partei Deutschlands* (Social Democratic Party of Germany) or "Social Democrats."

USPD: *Unabhaengige Sozialdemokratische Partei Deutschlands* (Independent Social Democratic Party of Germany).

KPD: *Kommunistische Partei Deutschlands* (Communist Party of Germany) or "Communists."

The last three parties are also referred to in the text as "Labor" or "Socialist" or "Marxist" parties.

For a brief survey of political parties in Germany see Neumann, "Political Parties—Germany" in *loc. cit.*

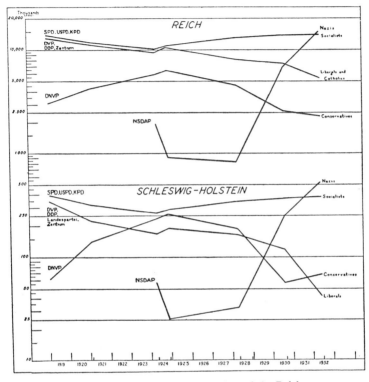

FIGURE 2. Party-Groups in Schleswig-Holstein and the Reich, 1919 to 1932.
Number of votes obtained. (Logarithmic scale)

TABLE 3. PERCENTAGES OF TOTAL VALID VOTE OBTAINED BY
SPECIFIED PARTIES IN SCHLESWIG-HOLSTEIN, 1919 TO JULY, 1932

	1919	1921	1924 (I)	1924 (II)	1928	1930	1932
NSDAP	—	—	7.4 *	2.7 **	4.0	27.0	51.0
Landvolk	—	—	—	—	0.3	3.8	0.0
DNVP	7.7	20.5	31.0	33.0	23.0	6.1	6.5
DVP	7.8	18.4	12.1	14.6	13.7	7.3	1.4
Zentrum	1.0	0.8	1.0	1.1	1.1	1.0	1.2
Landespartei	7.2	3.8	0.7	—	—	—	—
DDP	27.2	9.4	8.1	8.7	5.7	4.7	1.4
Other Parties	0.0	0.7	4.6	2.9	9.0	9.7	1.6
Socialists							
SPD	45.7	37.3	24.9	30.3	35.3	29.8	26.2
USPD	3.4	3.0	—	—	—	—	—
KPD	—	6.1	10.2	6.7	7.9	10.6	10.7

* *Deutsch-Voelkische Freiheitspartei.*
** *National-Sozialistische Freiheitspartei.*

During the final struggle for power, Schleswig-Holstein became the most outstanding scene of Nazi election victories: in 1930 the NSDAP reached here its highest percentage, 27 per cent of the total vote, and in July, 1932, Schleswig-Holstein was the only election district in which the NSDAP gained an absolute majority.

A comparison of the election results by rural and urban areas for the entire period shows clearly that the decline of loyalty to the Democratic regime was much more pronounced in the rural areas than in the urban communities.

While in 1919 those parties which more or less supported the new regime [71] obtained 88 per cent of the urban and 86 per cent of the rural vote, the support of the Democratic regime had declined by 1932 to about 37 per cent in the cities and 21 per cent in the rural communities.

The Nazis, while in the urban communities reaching only 44.8 per cent even in 1932, gained almost a two-thirds majority—63.8 per cent—in the rural communities.

[71] That is: DVP, *Landespartei*, DDP, and SPD.

TABLE 4. PERCENTAGES OF TOTAL VALID VOTE OBTAINED BY SPECIFIED PARTIES IN SCHLESWIG-HOLSTEIN, 1919 TO JULY, 1932, BY URBAN AND RURAL COMMUNITIES

	Total	NSDAP	Landvolk	DNVP	DVP	Landespartei	DDP	Center and minor parties	SPD	USPD	KPD
Urban											
1919	100	—	—	5.4	8.6	0.4	28.3	1.4	50.9	5.0	—
1920/21	100	—	—	16.2	19.6	1.2	10.5	1.9	39.8	3.2	7.6
1924 I	100	7.8	—	25.6	12.0	—	8.6	6.2	26.9	0.9	12.0
1924 II	100	2.9	—	27.8	14.5	—	9.2	3.9	32.8	0.4	8.5
1928	100	3.5	—	19.1	13.6	—	6.2	9.3	38.5	—	9.8
1930	100	23.2	0.6	5.3	8.4	—	5.7	8.7	33.1	—	13.1
1932	100	44.8	—	5.2	—	—	—	7.0	29.9	—	13.1
Rural											
1919	100	—	—	10.7	6.7	16.4	25.8	0.3	39.0	1.1	—
1920/21	100	—	—	28.6	16.1	8.6	7.3	0.6	33.0	2.6	3.2
1924 I	100	6.4	—	42.1	12.2	—	7.1	3.1	21.1	1.3	6.7
1924 II	100	2.3	—	43.4	14.9	—	7.8	2.4	25.4	0.5	3.3
1928	100	5.4	1.0	32.3	13.9	—	4.4	11.6	27.6	—	3.8
1930	100	35.1	10.7	7.9	4.8	—	2.5	11.1	22.8	—	5.1
1932	100	63.8	—	9.2	—	—	—	2.6	18.6	—	5.8

From a comparison of the combined SPD and KPD vote in rural and urban areas with the combined non-Socialist vote it appears that one major factor in the change of the political attitude of the rural population must have been the absence of as large a body of class-conscious voters among the rural laborers as was present in the cities.

Furthermore, if there was any threat at all of Communism, it certainly did not exist in the rural communities, where the KPD never obtained more than 6.7 per cent, while even in the cities the Communist vote remained at 13.1 per cent in the last two elections.

Two parties had an outspoken rural character: the *"Schleswig-Holsteinische Bauern und Landarbeiterdemo-*

kratie" or *"Landespartei"* in 1919 and 1921, and the *"Landvolkpartei"* in 1928 and 1930.

The Conservatives (DNVP), while receiving actually more votes in the cities than in rural areas, held through the entire period a considerably larger share of the rural vote than of the urban vote. The DVP, successor of the *Nationalliberale Partei,* on the other hand had its main absolute strength in the cities, although during the middle phase, from the stabilization of the *Reichsmark* by Stresemann in 1924 to the end of postwar prosperity in 1928, it commanded about equal proportions of the rural and of the urban vote.

The DDP, which inherited the tradition of the prewar radical Liberals or Progressives (*Freisinn*) became more and more an urban party.

On the whole one gains the impression of a stronger shift among the rural voters towards the "radical" parties of the right than among the urban voters. This becomes even more apparent if election results in single communities are considered: It was only in rural communities that the Nazis in 1932 reached from 70 per cent to 100 per cent of the votes cast, and there were numbers of such rural communities. On the whole the smaller the villages, the higher were the Nazi percentages. This inverse correlation between community size and Nazi vote is explained partly in terms of socio-economic structure of the smaller communities—the smaller, the more "rural" and the more agricultural—partly by the greater pressure of social control in a small community. Exceptions were found in some very small communities consisting of estates.

The distinctiveness of rural subregions in Schleswig-Holstein permits a comparative analysis of election data which can lead to an adequate insight into the factors that contributed to the change in party adherence among the rural people. The election results are published only by minor civil divisions (*Kreise*) and these do not constitute, in most cases, socially and economically homogeneous units. On the contrary, they cut across the boundaries of social subregions.[72] We shall therefore base our analysis primarily on votes by communities.[73]

If the percentages of the total vote obtained by the NSDAP in 1932 in each rural community were plotted on a map, we would find that the great majority of communities where the Nazis obtained more than 75 per cent of the vote were located on the *Geest*. Towards east and west the percentages decline; they are particularly low in the eastern area of large estates.

The distribution of the election results for the two Marxist parties (SPD and KPD) would show a complementary picture: These parties obtained largest percentages in the marshes and in the eastern hill zone, and low results on the *Geest*. Industrial villages and working class communities on the outskirts of the larger cities like Kiel, Neumuenster, Itzehoe show low Nazi and high Socialist and Communist percentages.

On the other hand, the Conservatives (DNVP), who were already very weak, in this election obtained relatively high percentages in communities in the marshes and in the eastern hill zone, while their score was generally

[72] The two Dithmarschen *Kreise*, for instance, comprise both marsh and *Geest* areas; Flensburg comprises eastern hill and *Geest* districts. The reason for such delineation of minor civil divisions is equalization of tax burdens—a pure *Geest Kreis* would be less capable of maintaining adequate public services, while a pure marsh *Kreis* would be at an unfair advantage.

[73] The data were obtained from the *Statistische Reichsamt*. We have to confine ourselves in parts of the study to selected *Kreise*, representing sectors of each of the three major zones and also comprising the most interesting smaller socio-cultural areas within each of these zones.

low on the *Geest*. Curiously enough, it was on the *Geest* that in 1919 the Liberal parties, that is the DDP and the *Schleswig-Holsteinische Landespartei,* had obtained the highest percentages in rural communities.

Reasons of economy forbade a thorough analysis of all elections by subregions or zones for the entire region. For certain selected *Kreise,*[74] representing sectors of each of the major zones, such analysis has been carried out. We are thus able to present time series of election results for the three subregions, for the major parties and party combinations.

In most elections and for the more important parties these data show obvious differences between the three major zones. Throughout the entire period, the Socialist parties have been comparatively strong in the marshes and the eastern hill zone, whereas they have been considerably weaker on the *Geest*. The Conservatives, on the other hand, were in most elections strongest in the hill zone in the east and weakest on the *Geest,* while they had intermediate successes in the marshes. The Nazis, with the exception of the election of December, 1924, when they did not obtain even 5 per cent in any region, were strongest on the *Geest* and weakest in the eastern hill zone, with the marshes in intermediate position. The Liberal parties show less consistency, but in the first two elections—the only ones in which they commanded very significant proportions of the rural vote—they were considerably stronger on the *Geest* than in the two other regions.

It seems then that the *Geest* has passed through a cycle

---

[74] These are: Schleswig, Flensburg, Eckernfoerde, Ploen, Oldenburg, Oldenburgischer Landesteil Luebeck, Rendsburg, Eiderstedt, Norder-und Suederdithmarschen. (For those underlined, community data were used in order to make division by major zone possible. The other *Kreise* were assigned in toto to their respective zones.)

TABLE 5. ELECTIONS TO THE REICHSTAG IN SCHLESWIG-HOLSTEIN COMMUNITIES WITH UNDER 2,000 POPULATION (RURAL COMMUNITIES), IN SELECTED MINOR CIVIL DIVISIONS (*Kreise*), BY MAJOR SUBREGIONS, 1919 TO 1932. PERCENTAGE OF TOTAL VOTE.

	Total	NSDAP	Landvolk	DNVP	DVP	Landespartei	DDP	Other Parties (non-Soc.)	SPD	USPD	KPD
Marsh											
1919	100	—	—	7.6	9.0	8.2	29.3	—	45.9	—	—
1921	100	—	—	29.0	20.1	5.0	6.4	0.1	27.6	6.4	5.4
1924 I	100	6.4	—	40.6	10.4	—	9.3	5.8	19.0	1.3	7.2
1924 II	100	3.1	—	41.4	11.5	—	11.5	3.4	24.7	—	4.4
1928	100	7.9	0.5	29.6	9.3	—	4.6	15.4	27.6	—	5.1
1930	100	41.2	7.0	5.3	3.1	—	2.8	6.8	25.5	—	8.3
1932 I	100	61.6	—	6.2	—	—	—	4.0	19.4	—	8.8
Geest											
1919	100	—	—	3.9	4.7	38.4	21.8	0.1	31.1	—	—
1921	100	—	—	25.3	13.0	27.5	5.7	0.9	22.1	3.5	2.0
1924 I	100	9.4	—	47.3	11.7	—	6.7	6.9	14.1	0.5	3.4
1924 II	100	2.4	—	49.9	18.1	—	8.6	3.3	16.1	—	1.6
1928	100	15.9	1.1	24.3	14.0	—	3.6	21.7	17.5	—	1.9
1930	100	45.9	14.2	3.7	3.7	—	3.0	11.6	14.7	—	3.2
1932 I	100	78.7	—	3.8	—	—	—	4.5	9.7	—	3.3
Hill Zone											
1919	100	—	—	15.8	6.3	14.3	21.7	0.3	39.6	2.0	—
1921	100	—	—	28.2	15.6	6.2	7.8	0.4	34.6	4.9	2.3
1924 I	100	5.5	—	38.7	13.7	—	6.7	2.8	24.0	1.0	7.6
1924 II	100	1.9	—	40.9	15.7	—	6.9	2.0	29.2	—	3.4
1928	100	2.0	0.4	32.7	15.0	—	4.3	10.0	32.6	—	3.0
1930	100	24.3	10.4	10.9	6.1	—	5.2	10.4	27.8	—	4.9
1932	100	57.1	—	10.0	—	—	—	4.9	21.4	—	6.6

Marsh = Eiderstedt, North and South Dithmarschen.
Geest = Kreis Rendsburg, Flensburg, Schleswig, North and South Dithmarschen.
Hill Zone = Flensburg, Schleswig, Eckernfoerde, Ploen, Oldenburg, Landesteil Luebeck (of freestate of Oldenburg).
Some communities on the edge of marsh and *Geest* and in the marshes along the Eider river have been disregarded.

from 65 per cent Liberals in 1919, to 50 per cent Conservatives in 1924, and almost 80 per cent Nazis in 1932. Variations in the other two zones were not so great. Before we attempt an explanation of these differences, we will have to consider briefly the main factors affecting political behavior of rural people.

Every party tries to appeal to as broad a public as possible. The success of such appeal will depend on the intensity of class antagonism and on the width of social distance between status groups. Where class lines are not clearly visible by objective criteria of source and size of income, where social mobility is great and where other factors tend to obliterate economic class distinctions in daily social intercourse, there the political parties are more likely to expand beyond class boundaries than in areas where people think very definitely in terms of class and status.

The political choices of rural people, especially of farmers, are determined less by ideologies and general political ideals than by the weighing of concrete advantages and disadvantages to be expected from the rule of one or the other party. The readiness of the farmer to support any particular government depends largely on the expectation that the government's policy will produce tangible results for agriculture. The more commercialized the farming in a given region, the more will the farmers' prosperity depend on oscillations of the market prices of staple products. In other words, the more commercialized and the more specialized the farming in a region, the more will the political attitude of the farmers be influenced by the vagaries of business cycles and of structural changes in the general economic system of the country.

On the other hand, everybody familiar with party constellations in the United States will know that such sensitivity can be modified by the firmness of regional political traditions. In a region where a broad and influential local class has for a long time been leading in certain political parties, any new party will find it difficult to win support in this class and to break its influence on or control over the other classes in the region.

But where such leadership has been lacking and where a class hitherto not vocal in political life is coming of age, there the chances for a new political movement to win adherents will be more favorable.

We shall now consider the development in each of the three major zones separately.

The *marshes* are the most commercialized agricultural region in Schleswig-Holstein. The coastal lowlands of Dithmarschen and Eiderstedt especially have a tradition of more than two centuries of commercial farming. Labor relations in the coastal marshes have long since been known for their contractual character and for their lack of community spirit. The deep cleavage between rich and poor, between farmer and cottager or laborer, is emphasized by the settlement pattern: the farmers live on single farmsteads with spacious buildings in the midst of their fields and pastures; the poor, the working class people in villages and in small line-settlements along the sea dikes and the edge of the *Geest*.

Similar conditions are found in the Elbmarshes; but farming here is more diversified, and the wealthy farmers are perhaps more tradition-bound than those in Eiderstedt and Dithmarschen. However, the segregation of the rural social classes and the dependence on markets are the same.

The particular nature of marsh farming, which requires little continuous work on the part of the farmowners, made them available for public offices, and even permitted some of them to practice the legal profession or to engage in business activities. Thus the wealthy among the farmers constitute an old political ruling class.

Dithmarschen, however, is not entirely marsh; about half of its area lies on the *Geest*. The *Geest* people were until recently much poorer than the marsh farmers and did not play any leading role in the public life of the region. Economically, the two parts are closely inter-related, because the *Geest* farmers raise the cattle which are bought by the marsh farmers for fattening on their rich pastures. The same interdependence of marsh and *Geest* and the same social distinctions exist farther north in North Friesland (Kreis Husum and Kreis Suedtondern).

Before 1918 the rich marsh farmers were traditionally attached to the *Nationalliberale* or to the *Freikonservative* party, while the smaller farmers, the middle classes in the small towns and also the working class people adhered to the *Freisinnige* or to the Progressive party.

The elections for the National Constitutional Assembly in 1919 resulted in a very strong majority in favor of the new regime; in the rural marsh communities of Eiderstedt and Dithmarschen 83.4 per cent of the vote was cast for the DDP, *Landespartei,* SPD, and USPD. About half of these went to the two Marxist parties, a clear indication of the intensity of class cleavage.

While the Marxist parties held their strength fairly well from 1920 on (receiving between 30 per cent and 37 per cent of the votes in the rural communities of the marsh areas in Eiderstedt and Dithmarschen together, and between 34 per cent and 44 per cent in the marshes of Dithmarschen alone) the Liberal parties declined sharply and gave way to the Conservatives, who in turn lost the top rank to the Nazis.

The decline of the Liberal parties in the rural marsh communities of Dithmarschen and Eiderstedt from 46.5 per cent of the vote in 1919 to 9.2 per cent in 1930 signifies a complete change in the political attitude of the marsh farmers.

On the other hand, it is interesting and highly significant that since 1928 the NSDAP scored considerably less
in the marshes of Dithmarschen than on the *Geest.* Also,
the *proportion* of the total vote for the non-Marxist or
"middle class" parties which went to the Nazis was on
the whole smaller in the marshes of Dithmarschen than
on the *Geest,* although in some earlier elections the relation had been the reverse.

TABLE 6. RADICALIZATION OF "MIDDLE CLASS" PARTIES IN RURAL
COMMUNITIES OF DITHMARSCHEN BY SUBREGIONS

	Percentage of middle class party votes cast for NSDAP		Percentage of total vote cast for middle class parties	
	Marsh	*Geest*	*Marsh*	*Geest*
1924 I	10.2	7.0	69.4	84.9
1924 II	5.5	3.6	68.7	85.8
1928	16.1	41.1	63.3	82.4
1930	66.5	67.4	63.6	82.0
1932	87.1	92.1	69.0	87.7

The marsh showed thus less solidarity of political opinion than the *Geest,* but on the other hand also a slightly
greater stability of political opinion.

Dithmarschen and the Steinburg and Pinneberg Kreise
which comprise most of the Elbmarshes were early
strongholds of the organized NSDAP. However, it is
significant that the communities in which the Nazis had
strong organizations were located either on the *Geest*
or in the border zone between marsh and *Geest* and not
in the marsh proper.

Nevertheless, the radicalization both of the labor class
and of the farmers in the marshes remains remarkable.
An explanation may be attempted in terms of increasing
economic insecurity rather than of actual suffering from
the agricultural depression. The marsh farmer has always
been inclined to incur great speculative risks: cattle grazing and cabbage farming involve a gambling element—
the enormous gains of one year may be cancelled by the

losses of the next; sometimes the entire market value of the farm may be earned by a single good crop, while the heavy demand for short term credit may plunge the farmer deeply into debt in the next year. During the period of cheap bank loans after the First World War, many of the marsh farmers had incurred heavy debts, and not always for production purposes. When the markets collapsed and credit became difficult to obtain—that is, from 1929 on—these farmers found themselves in a very critical financial situation.

In the Elbmarshes the decline of horse breeding (because of motorization and reduction of army demands) and of certain rural industries (the raising and processing of willows for basket-making) as well as the repeated crises in the hog fattening industry in 1926–1927 and 1929–1930, accounted among the farmers, large and small, for rising discontent with the existing political conditions. This paved the way for the Nazis.

On the other hand, the Marxist parties obtained support not only from the workers and artisans in the small coastal towns but also from the fishermen who were quite severely hit by the depression, and therefore began more than ever to feel their dependence on the canning companies as employers and creditors. A similar radicalization of fishermen was observed on the east coast on the island of Maasholm.

The *eastern hill zone* comprises two different types of subregions: Angeln, the Isle of Fehmarn and the Probstei (a group of villages in the northern tip of the Ploen Kreis) are farmers' districts, while the rest is characterized by the prevalence of large estates. These estates dominate especially in the Ploen and Oldenburg Kreise. Agriculture in the entire region is well diversified, except for Fehmarn, where barley and wheat are the predominating crops. Angeln has an especially well-balanced system of family farming, with grain production, dairying, cattle and horse breeding and hog raising well integrated.

The social stratification in Angeln was more complex than in the coastal marshes: While the big farmers constituted the leading and ruling class, there was a substantial class of smaller farmers and cottagers, sometimes settled in small communities which are old offshoots of the original villages; finally there was a class of day-laborers and of hired hands. Labor relations were stable, with a residue of patriarchalism. In spite of distinct stratification neighborhood relations were strong and well institutionalized. The class structure of Fehmarn was more like that in the marshes.

Until 1919 the large estates in east Holstein resembled in social structure those in Mecklenburg and other regions east of the Elbe. However, the concentration of farming operations in the hands of the landlord had not been as far advanced as in those other regions. There existed a co-operation between the main estate with its cottagers and wage laborers and the often quite well-to-do tenant farmers in the villages, most of whom had held the same farm through many generations.[75] Land reform legislation after 1919 resulted in the transformation of tenants into owners on the former tenant land of the estates and in the resettlement of some of the former cottagers with public financial support.[76]

Thus, while the old upper classes of estate owners and

[75] Either as *Zeitpaechter* (long-term tenants) or *Erbpaechter* (hereditary tenants). These forms of tenancy were the substitutes for serfdom which had been abolished at the end of the 18th century, that is, much earlier than in Prussia.

[76] Resettlement activity in Schleswig-Holstein was strong; from 1919 to 1935 (that is, chiefly until 1932) more than the acreage which the province was legally required to make available (103.4 per cent) for resettlement purposes was actually made available, and 5,899 new and 1,542 "Anlieger" farms were established. (*Statistisches Jahrbuch fuer das Deutsche Reich, 1936*, p. 82.)

big farmers were, thanks to their diversified economy, fairly safe against the vicissitudes of the postwar agricultural cycles, there had come into existence a layer of new proprietors of small, and often too small, farms who were committed to fixed interest and annuity payments to public finance institutions—a situation which became quite threatening when agricultural prices began to drop in the late twenties and credit became more difficult to obtain.

Politically, east Holstein before 1918 had been dominated by the owners of estates. These adhered to the Conservative or *Freikonservative* party, while the *Social Democrats* and the Progressives competed for the vote of the agricultural laborers, the small farmers and the tenants, and also the lower middle class in the small towns. The control of the landlords over the villages, however, constituted a severe handicap for the democratic parties.

After the revolution of 1918, the discontent with the politically obsolete system of tenancy resulted in strong majorities for the Socialist and Democratic parties. Very soon, however, the Conservatives (DNVP) became the leading "middle class" party in east Holstein, strongly opposed by the combined Marxist parties. When finally, in 1930 and 1932, the Conservatives gave way to the Nazis, the latter obtained their strongest successes in the farmers' areas of east Holstein and not in the areas of large estates, where both the Marxists and the Conservatives preserved their strength somewhat better.[77] (Table 7.)

Angeln was before 1918 politically dominated by an upper class of rich and often well-educated farmers who, not being quite so conservative as the large landlords,

[77] While the relative resistance of the landed aristocracy to Nazism is being emphasized here, it should not be forgotten that the Conservative landowners did nothing to prevent the rise to power of the Nazis and that they lent them their support in various ways.

TABLE 7. ELECTION RESULTS IN RURAL COMMUNITIES IN THE
EASTERN HILL ZONE

Type of Community	NSDAP		DNVP		SPD and KPD	
	1932	*1930*	*1932*	*1930*	*1932*	*1930*
Estates—prevalent						
Kreis Oldenburg	41.4	16.0	11.0	18.6	45.0	49.6
Kreis Ploen	45.3	18.8	9.8	15.3	42.4	46.5
Farmers' villages						
Isle of Fehmarn	47.0	23.9	8.6	16.7	41.8	44.3
Kreis Oldenburg	52.0	25.5	9.3	19.0	36.4	41.6
Kreis Ploen	52.2	23.9	10.9	16.7	33.9	36.1
Probstei	59.5	38.0	11.8	17.4	26.0	29.7
Kreis Eckernfoerde (mixed)	60.1	22.2	9.2	11.3	28.2	31.4
Angeln (farmers)	70.8	24.6	10.5	7.0	12.5	15.0

adhered to the *Nationalliberale* or to the *Freikonserva-tive* party. In 1919 the *Landespartei,* political creation of the *Bauernverein* which had many members among the smaller farmers in Angeln, emerged as the leading party, with 35.5 per cent of the total vote. The DDP was second with 27.9 per cent, and the DVP obtained 8 per cent —the three liberal parties together 71.4 per cent, or as much as the NSDAP scored in 1932. By 1924 the Conservatives had become the strongest party, with 43 per cent, which was about the average for Schleswig-Holstein. The Marxist parties were weak throughout the entire period but formed a rather firm block of about 3,500 votes. The important feature of the political development in Angeln and the factor which retarded the rise of the NSDAP was the strong position of the right-wing Liberals, the DVP. This party, successor to the *National-liberale Partei,* obtained in 1928 and 1930 almost twice as large a percentage of all votes as in the average of Schleswig-Holstein. Another factor which retarded the penetration by the Nazis was the strength of the *Landvolkpartei* in 1930.

A firm political tradition, a definite social stratification, and at the same time a well-developed agricultural ladder which facilitated social climbing, a well-balanced agriculture and a sound farm-credit situation, together with the moderate temper and the religiousness of the Anglian, may account for the tardiness of the region in giving in to the oncoming wave of Nazism. Even in 1933 the party organization was reported to be much weaker in Angeln than in most other sections of Schleswig-Holstein. However, the high degree of political solidarity which distinguishes family farm areas from areas of large estates made it possible for the NSDAP to obtain in Angeln in 1932 the highest percentages of the total vote in the entire hill zone.[78]

Of all three major zones, the *Geest* showed the greatest instability of political opinion. Here, on the sandy and moory soils, the tradition of past poverty lingered on, and the standards of living of the rural people were still decidedly simpler than in the other two regions.

---

[78] A particularly striking case of farmers-village solidarity was revealed in Schwackendorf, a village in Angeln. Here almost the entire population voted NSDAP in 1932, while in the neighboring village of Gelting the Nazis obtained only slightly more than half of the votes. Local informants stated that in Schwackendorf the leading farmers had agreed among themselves to join the NSDAP in a body. The important point is that this action was taken primarily because the farmers wanted to maintain the political unanimity of the village, out of a spirit of neighborliness. Gelting on the other hand comprises an estate, belonging to a Catholic family; consequently both the Socialists and the "other parties" (including the Center party) remained here relatively strong.

Total number of voters in 1932	Schwackendorf 180	Gelting 325
SPD and KPD	3.9%	18.8%
DNVP	0.6	13.5
Other parties	1.1	12.0
NSDAP	94.4	55.7
Total	100.0	100.0

Also, the *Geest* farmer was less commercially minded, less given to risky business transactions than the marsh farmer. On the other hand, agriculture was not so well balanced on the *Geest* as in Angeln or Ostholstein; the preponderance of animal husbandry made the *Geest* farmer dependent on the demand, by the grazing farmers in the marshes, for young cattle (*magervieh*), that is, ultimately on the beef cattle market in Hamburg or the Rhineland, and also on the hog market with its well-known cycles. This was especially true of the northern *Geest* while in the south, in the hinterland of the metropolitan cities of Hamburg, Kiel, and Luebeck, milk production and truck farming were more developed and furnished a fairly steady cash income. Needs for production credit were generally less than in the other zones.

The social structure of the *Geest* villages was less complex than the village structure in the other zones; there were very few large estates; and, since most of the farms are small enough to be operated by the family and a few hired servants and occasional day laborers, there existed in these villages no broad class of agricultural laborers. The few small cottagers were usually accepted as part of the village community. Differences in wealth were not emphasized as status-distinctions. Neighborhood relations were strong, and there was no spatial segregation of rich and poor. Thus, the *Geest* villages presented a much higher degree of community solidarity than any of the other zones.

However, until 1918 the *Geest* had been lacking political leadership, nor had the *Geest* farmers participated in the rural political leadership of the region which rested with the marsh farmers or the eastern landlords (*Gutsbesitzer*), none of whom accepted even the well-to-do *Geest* farmer as their social equal. Although the *Geest* people had never known serfdom, there was no old tradition of self-government as in the marshes. The prevailing political tendency before 1918 had been that typical of the "small" people in Schleswig-Holstein—Progressive Liberalism. About 1918 there emerged on the *Geest* an organization of farmers which later on formed the foundation of the short-lived *Landespartei*—for the first time a movement of *Geest* farmers, led by men of their own group.[79]

It seems very likely that this lack of an old, experienced political leadership, together with the relative absence of class antagonism and class distinctions in the *Geest* villages, accounts for the completeness of political shifts in this zone. The social structure prevented the development of a strong bloc of Marxist voters in most of the rural *Geest* villages, except in some rural industrial communities,[80] and this weakness of the Marxist parties

---

[79] See Chapter III.

[80] A good illustration of the relation between social structure and political constellation is offered by the two industrial villages of Muensterdorf and Laegerdorf on a *Geest* "island" south of Itzehoe (Kreis Steinburg). Since the comparison of these villages is suited to convey an idea of the way in which the regional analysis was pursued into local detail (in the original study), the findings may be briefly presented as an example. Both are former farmers' villages whose population at the time of the investigation consisted largely of workers in the near-by stone quarries and a cement factory in Laegerdorf. (P. Hermberg, *Die Bevoelkerung des Kirchspiels Muensterdorf* [Dissertation, Kiel, 1913].) A third village on this *Geest* "island," Daegeling, was still predominantly an agricultural village. While in Daegeling the relation between "labor" and "middle class" votes in 1919 was almost 50:50, the two industrial villages had very considerable majorities of the Marxist parties. This relation had not been changed in 1932 in Muensterdorf and Laegerdorf; however, within the "middle class" bloc a considerable shift toward the Nazis had taken place, and in Laegerdorf the radicalization of the labor vote was noteworthy. This difference in the political attitude of the labor class in the two villages may be explained mainly by the much higher degree of migratory mobility among the workers in Laegerdorf; for, a high turnover in the labor force

gave the Nazis a much wider margin than in the other zones. The strongly developed sense of community solidarity made it easier to swing the vote of an entire village towards a new party, than in the marshes where a more developed individualism and sharper class distinctions operated as retarding factors.

We may then, in concluding our regional survey, state tentatively that, while the decline of liberalism and the growth of the counter-revolutionary parties were conditioned by the general factor of economic distress, the subregional differentials between the strength of the various parties were primarily determined by the social structure of the communities rather than directly by economic factors.

However, the structure of agriculture in marsh and *Geest* made these subregions especially sensitive. All of

---

makes union organization difficult and therefore impedes effective organization of a labor party that, like the SPD, is based on labor unions. In Daegeling, where the Marxists obtained almost 50 per cent of the vote in 1919, a complete reversal occurred: the middle parties were wiped out by 1932 and the Nazis dominated the community with 79 per cent of the vote against 20 per cent Marxists.

	Percentage of valid votes cast for specified parties						
	SPD	KPD or USPD	Marxists	DDP	Landespartei	Right DNVP, DVP, etc.	NSDAP	Other parties
Muensterdorf								
1919	70.8	0.2	71.0	17.3	0.8	10.7	—	0.2
1932	53.5	13.8	67.3	1.3	—	3.0	26.9	1.5
Laegerdorf								
1919	76.6	0.9	77.5	17.4	—	4.6	—	0.5
1932	26.8	43.7	70.5	0.8	—	2.6	24.0	2.1
Daegeling								
1919	x	x	49.5	15.9	18.7	15.9	—	—
1932	x	x	20.1	0.9	—	—	78.7	0.8

their products are subject to a great elasticity of demand, and all of them are perishable. Their prices are apt to fall as soon as the purchasing power of the urban consumers is reduced. The two slumps in hog prices in 1926–1927 and 1929–1930 affected particularly the *Geest* farmers. The year 1930–1931 brought the slump in cattle prices which most severely affected marsh and *Geest* farmers; in the next year cabbage prices declined, and at the same time the crops in Dithmarschen failed. These developments came on top of the disparity in farm and industrial prices and the tightening of the credit situation which had begun about 1929.

More specifically it may be said that the classes particularly susceptible for Nazism were neither the rural nobility and big farmers nor the rural proletariat, but rather the small farm proprietors, very much the rural equivalent of the lower middle class or petty bourgeoisie (*Kleinbuergertum*) which formed the backbone of the NSDAP in the cities.[81]

This hypothesis will now be tested by a series of correlations between party strength and socio-economic factors.[82]

[81] The Nazis had an especially strong appeal to these classes because of the combination in their ideology of the resentment of the small property owner, farmer and manufacturer, and also of certain elements among the employees, against "big business" on the one hand and against the rising power of labor on the other hand. The relation between the Nazi movement and the middle classes has been treated frequently; the most thorough analysis of the subject is to be found in Geiger, *op. cit.*

[82] During the first years of social unrest among farmers in Schleswig-Holstein, that is in 1928 and 1929, many observers believed that the *Landvolk* and Nazi movements in the region were typical debtors' movements. There can be little doubt that a very large proportion of the farmers who voted the Nazi ticket did so because they hoped for a moratorium or a permanent abolition of all debts. Statistical proof of this statement was however not obtainable because the only reliable data on farm debts were for 1928 and could not be classified by major social zones.

From the previous discussion it appears that at the end of the period the Conservatives were weakest where the Nazis were strongest and that the Nazis were relatively weak where the Conservatives were strong. On the other hand, the Social Democrats and Communists had their greatest rural following where the Conservatives were also strong. This would indicate that, where the actual social conditions in the rural areas came close to the Nazi ideal of "community," the NSDAP obtained a stronger support than in those rural areas where a sharp distinction existed between landlords and laborers. In fact, a correlation of the votes obtained in 1932 by the conservative DNVP and of the combined SPD and KPD respectively in eighteen predominantly rural *Kreise*, after exclusion of towns of 10,000 or more population, results in a strong positive coefficient (plus .91). On the other hand, the correlation for the same *Kreise* between percentages of votes obtained by the NSDAP and by the DNVP is negative (minus .89).

We shall now test our tentative assumption that the class structure of the farm population has influenced the election results. If it is true, we should find strong positive correlations between the Conservative and also the Socialist vote and the percentage of agricultural workers gainfully employed on estates and large farms on the one hand, and on the other hand also strong positive correlations between the Nazi vote and the percentage of workers in agriculture gainfully employed on small and medium farms.[83]

Since certain small tenants' and cottagers' farms which

[83] The percentage of all agricultural workers gainfully occupied on farms of specified size was used rather than the percentage of all farms in specified size classes, because the former indicator has a closer relation to the number of voters.

economically belong to estates or furnish the labor for them are enumerated as separate agricultural enterprises, it seemed advisable to combine the percentages of persons engaged on very small farms with those engaged on the largest size class. Furthermore, only the vote in rural areas of eighteen civil divisions was considered.

The results for several elections are presented in Table 8. The findings appear to be quite consistent and in agreement with our assumptions.

It appears that the Nazis had in 1932 really succeeded the former liberal parties, like the *Landespartei* and Democratic party, as the preferred party among the small

TABLE 8. SCHLESWIG-HOLSTEIN *—CORRELATIONS BETWEEN PERCENTAGES OF TOTAL VALID VOTE OBTAINED IN RURAL COMMUNITIES OF 18 MINOR CIVIL DIVISIONS, AND PERCENTAGES OF ALL GAINFUL WORKERS IN AGRICULTURE ** ON FARMS OF SPECIFIED SIZE

Parties and Years of Election		Farm Size Classes		
		Small Farms— 2–20 ha (Kleinbauern)	Large Farms— 20–100 ha (Grossbauern)	Estates and Very Small Farms— 100 or More and Less than 2 ha
Socialists	1919	—.97	—.43	+.88
SPD, USPD,	1921	—.98	—.45	+.95
KPD	1930	—.92	—.43	+.92
	1932	—.80	—.40	+.83
Democrats and	1919	+.89	+.52	—.94
Landespartei	1921	+.80	+.34	—.77
Conservatives	1919	—.70	—.34	+.76
DNVP	1921	—.19	—.04	+.02
	1930	—.60	—.49	+.61
	1932	—.80	—.40	+.83
Landvolk	1930	+.59	+.26	—.64
NSDAP and Landvolk	1930	+.79	+.45	—.82
NSDAP	1930	+.43	+.26	—.43
	1932	+.85	+.49	—.89

* Province of Schleswig-Holstein and part of Oldenburg.
** Landwirtschaftliche Erwerbstaetige.

farmers (2–20 ha). The larger farmers (20–100 ha) appear to have been less definitely committed to any of the major reactionary parties or to any of the liberal parties. However, the low correlation coefficients are partly due to the influence of the labor vote in large farm areas.

Very significant is the fact that, in cases where positive correlations are found with the Nazis, the correlations with the Socialist parties are negative, and vice versa.[84]

The analysis of the relations between party strength and class structure can also be carried on by comparing data from the occupational statistics with election results. This has been done for eighteen *Kreise*, excluding cities of 10,000 or more population.[85]

[84] The correlations presented are a selection of a larger series of correlations with a variety of classifications of gainful workers by farm sizes and combinations of parties. The selected correlations, though not the strongest throughout, appeared to reveal the sociologically most significant relations. The correlations were computed by Spearman's rank correlation method $(\rho = 1 - \dfrac{6\,\Sigma D^2}{N(N^2 - 1)})$.

[85] The use of community election results would have been preferable, but had to be discarded since the occupational data were available for minor civil divisions only. Another serious handicap is the heterogeneity of the socio-economic classes in the occupational statistics. The class of owners, etc., comprises, for instance, owners of large estates and small farmers, the poor tradesman, and the rich factory owner. The class of salaried employees comprises managerial and expert technical personnel with high incomes and the salesgirls in ten-cent stores if they happen to be paid by the month instead of by the day or week. Domestic servants are classified separately.

The German statistics distinguish between (1) *Erwerbspersonen* or persons in gainful occupations inclusive of unemployed persons and (2) *Berufszugehoerige* or the total number of persons depending on a certain occupation or industry (that is, *Erwerbspersonen* and their dependents not in full time gainful occupations). The text refers to *Berufszugehoerige*.

The occupational statistics distinguish between the following major socio-economic classes: (a) owners, proprietors, and other persons in directing positions, (b) salaried employees and officials, (c) wage earners, and (m) family members employed in the business or on the farm of the head of the household; the latter class is important as an element of small farm and middle class economy.

Three sets of correlations have been computed for each of the major industrial divisions and a fourth for agriculture alone.

The first set tests the association of political parties with the degree of middle class character of the minor civil divisions as measured by the proportion of proprietors of farms or other business enterprises in the total population. The fourth set, which is computed for agriculture and forestry only, is merely a test of the first—the assumption being that the larger the combined proportion of proprietors and family workers in the total population, the more outspoken the lower middle class (*kleinbaeuerliche* or *kleinbuergerliche*) character of the *Kreis*.

The second set tests the association of the party votes with the proportion of wage earners in the total population—an indicator of the political attitude of the rural and rural industrial labor class.

The third set was computed as a test of the second, on the assumption that the larger the proportion of wage earners and salaried employees in relation to the owners, the more distinct would be the working class as the predominating element on the one hand and the class of entrepreneurs on the other, that is, the more concentrated would be agriculture or industry or commerce in large enterprises and therefore the weaker would be the "middle class" of small farmers and small businessmen.

The results, presented in Table 9, confirm very well the expectations. They show clearly the association of the Nazi strength with the middle classes, and of the strength of the Socialists with the prevalence of the labor class.

The results also show how the vote of the farmers shifted from the Liberals to the Conservatives and finally in 1932 to the Nazis. The shift of the vote of the proprietor class in industry and commerce and in all industrial divisions together is also strikingly expressed in the strong positive correlations, first in 1921 with the Liberals, then in 1924 and 1930 with the Conservatives, and finally in 1932 with the Nazis.

On the other hand, the steadiness of the correlations between the percentages of wage earners and the parties is also impressive. It indicates that, on the whole, labor must have adhered to the Socialist parties. Only the Conservatives at the beginning and at the end of the period seem to have gained some support among agricultural workers, unless the positive correlations (between Conservative votes and percentages of workers) which are very low at any rate, are merely the result of "symbiosis" of agricultural labor with Conservative landlords.

This latter assumption seems to be confirmed by the third set of correlations in each industrial division. The larger the ratio of employees (wage and salary earners) to employers, the stronger the Socialist parties and the weaker all others, including the Nazis.

We may then say that the Nazis did not gain much ground among the workers, especially not where large scale enterprises prevailed, be it in agriculture and forestry, or in industry, commerce, and transportation. Both among the farmers and the non-agricultural rural population the middle strata (of small farmers and small entrepreneurs), and to some extent also the agricultural work-

SCHLESWIG-HOLSTEIN—CORRELATIONS BETWEEN PERCENTAGES OF VOTES OBTAINED BY PARTIES IN 18 MINOR CIVIL DIVISIONS (CITIES OF 10,000 OR MORE POPULATION EXCLUDED) WITH PERCENTAGES OF POPULATION IN SPECIFIED SOCIO-ECONOMIC CLASSES (BERUFSZUGEHOERIGE) BY MAJOR INDUSTRIAL DIVISIONS

Party	Year	Agriculture, Forestry, Fishery				Industry and Handicraft			Industry, Commerce and Transportation			All Industrial Divisions including Public Services, Domestic Service, etc.		
		Proprietors (a)	a+m	Wage earners (c)	$\frac{b+c}{a}$	a	c	$\frac{b+c}{a}$	a	c	$\frac{b+c}{a}$	a	c	$\frac{b+c}{a}$
Socialists SPD, USPD, KPD	1921	−.84	−.88	+.86	+.85	−.68	+.65	+.68	−.70	+.62	+.64	−.93	+.95	+.93
	1932	−.79	−.78	+.77	+.77	−.84	+.82	+.84	−.81	+.69	+.80	−.94	+.88	+.94
Liberals DVP, DDP, Landespartei; Center	1921	+.81	+.85	−.77	−.85	+.50	−.48	−.50	+.54	−.53	−.49	+.84	−.86	−.96
Conservatives DNVP	1921	−.20	±0.0	+.22	+.20	+.23	−.24	−.23	+.15	−.31	−.17	+.08	+.07	+.10
	1924 II	+.40	+.45	−.41	−.39	+.68	−.66	−.68	+.57	−.71	−.59	+.52	−.47	−.52
	1932	−.26	−.28	+.31	+.28	+.09	−.08	−.09	−.09	−.15	−.06	+.02	+.12	+.12
Landvolk	1930	+.67	+.69	−.64	−.68	+.58	−.30	−.53	+.49	−.39	−.26	+.74	−.77	−.74
NSDAP	1930	+.37	+.43	−.43	−.40	+.32	−.39	−.31	+.24	−.40	−.67	+.36	−.38	−.64
	1932	+.76	+.79	−.78	−.76	+.71	−.69	−.70	+.63	−.53	−.64	+.83	−.79	−.69

Explanation of occupational classifications:

a = proprietors
m = family members employed on farm
c = wage earners

b = salaried employees

$\frac{b+c}{a}$ = ratio of all employees to proprietors

ers in family farm areas, have been most susceptible to Nazism; while the landlords and big farmers were more reluctant to cast their vote for Hitler. The workers on large estates, and especially the industrial and commercial wage earners, have been most resistant to the Nazi movement. The change from Liberalism to Nazism, or from support of the democratic regime to support of the opposition, has been most radical just in those middle layers of rural society, which in the period before 1918 had been strong adherents of progressive Liberalism. The comparative strength of these middle strata in the rural society of the *Geest* and their relative weakness and lesser political influence in the two other regions explain very well the regional differences in political behavior observed in the beginning of this discussion.

In concluding our analysis at this point we may say that the "ecological" approach has led us to fairly definite and apparently well-supported ideas about the political conduct of the various strata or classes in the rural society of our region. It may seem strange that the agricultural workers and other wage earners, held firmly to one of two Socialist parties while the middle and upper strata, especially the supposedly ideal backbone of democracy—the family farmer—swayed from left to right like reeds in the wind and finally supported a political movement which was diametrically opposed to their own political tradition.

The contrast in the political conduct of the two classes is largely conditioned by the possession of a firm faith, a political philosophy on the part of the workers, and by the loss of faith in existing political institutions and the development of a political opportunism of fundamentally materialistic nature on the part of the middle classes.

The classes of *Kleinbuerger* and *Kleinbauern*, both survivals of the pre-capitalistic age and both in a process of social decomposition, were ideologically opposed to capitalism but also to the proletarian labor movement. Many among them saw in the Hitler movement the promise of a new community-of-the-people in which class differences would be minimized but private property of land and capital preserved. Among the big farmers and *Gutsbesitzer* as well as among manufacturers, businessmen, and the rest of the *Buergertum* a more sophisticated attitude towards the Hitler movement prevailed.[86]

[86] They probably thought like one of them, a marsh farmer and lawyer who had read Tönnies, who said in an interview when I pointed out to him the contradiction between Nazi Totalitarianism and the community consciousness and tradition of self-government in his own Eiderstedt: "We know that of course. But we believe that in the Third Reich we, the farmers, will be so strong a power that we can shape it as we desire."

V

CONCLUSIONS AND INTERPRETATIONS

OUR analysis has shown that, as long as a free expression of political opinions was possible, the National Socialists were opposed by sociologically well-defined majorities in most parts of Schleswig-Holstein, as in other regions of Germany. And even where, as in certain rural sections of Schleswig-Holstein, they obtained strong majorities, they did so only after long years of effort when despair had seized large sectors of the population.

We have also seen that by and large the industrial and agricultural labor classes proved to be relatively inaccessible to the Nazis and that the rural and urban upper classes, although in sympathy with the general counter-revolutionary direction of National Socialism, kept for a long time, in their majority, aloof of Hitler's brown forces, whom they rather hoped to exploit for their own purposes.

The main mass support came, as we have clearly shown, from the middle layers of society, from those *Kleinbauern* and *Kleinbuerger* who in the past had adhered to political ideas very different from those characteristic of the Nazi creed. We have seen how the National Socialists, by appealing to certain deep-seated resentments and sentiments, by skillfully utilizing economic interests and, we may add, by concealing their own ultimate aims, gradually won the support of these classes.

Where we discovered elements related to the Nazi creed in the earlier ideology of these classes, we found

that these ideas were associated with sentiments and attitudes very different from and even opposed to the aggres-
sive, imperialistic, anti-humanitarian, and anti-Christian
spirit of the original leader-circle of the Hitler movement. We found a striking absence of war-of-revenge
sentiments, even an attitude of conciliation with the
project of a new federative European order which would
weaken the strength of national states. Where the idea
of a new "community" arose in these middle classes, it
sprang from a contemplative, quietistic, and sometimes
romantic, attitude; the very notions of bigness and power
were rather despised. In listening to these professions of
a new faith in the people, one is reminded of Tönnies
and Charles Horton Cooley rather than of Hitler and
Goebbels. The ideology of the *Kleinbauern* and *Kleinbuerger* in the early years of the period was a rather radical reaction against the war and the powers that had been
responsible for its conduct. It was a reaction against government regimentation as well as a reaction against years
of military rule. To be sure, some of these ideas were not
realistic. They were not the ideas of an old ruling class.
These ideas and sentiments were rather the expression
of the mentality of classes that had not had much experience in active and leading participation in the political
life of the nation. It was this lack of political experience,
combined with the resentment of the small farmer and
small businessman against the "big-shots," in combination with more temporary factors, that aided the Nazis
in winning the support of these classes. Since a large part,
if not the majority, of them were living in comparatively
homogeneous communities with a strong sense of solidarity, the Nazis were able to swing the entire vote in many
of these villages, resorting, as everywhere else, to a great
deal of intimidation.

These classes then were attracted to Nazism by the egalitarian temper and by promises of desired economic policies, rather than by the specific fascistic elements.

It was among the young people that the idea of leadership developed, and it was particularly among the young salaried employees, the young agricultural technicians and experts, that this idea was combined with the cry for a strong and centralized government. Youth and politically young groups, that is groups without experience and tradition in the conduct of public affairs, are most easily swayed and captured by the kind of emotional demagogery in which the Nazis very soon achieved mastership.

The conservative politicians and their supporters among the rural and urban upper classes, seeing in the Hitler movement primarily a disturbing but fundamentally wholesome rebirth of nationalist sentiments, which they felt should be patronized to some extent, committed the fatal error of underestimating the dynamic forces of self-perpetuation in any such mass movement as well as the strength of the will to power among its leaders.

We know of course that after Hitler's ascent to power, large masses of hitherto indifferent or undecided people in all social strata—but mainly in the middle and upper strata of the *Buergertum*—were seemingly converted to the new political creed. However, in many cases these conversions were nothing but a rationalization of conduct that was motivated by ambition or fear. The conversion usually took a gradual course: the convert would find himself in agreement with certain aims of the new regime while rejecting others, only to find out when it was too late, that the very nature of the regime prohibited such mental reservations.

We may predict that these late converts—the *Maerz-*

gefallenen and those of even later vintage—will not be very faithful once the regime has started to crumble. The number of these late converts cannot be inferred from the increase in Nazi votes after the seizure of power; this will be obvious to anybody who has seen how those "elections" were conducted. Only very few of those who were opposed to the Hitler regime had the sense and the courage to engage in a futile protest by voting against Hitler in elections, the results of which were generally considered as falsifications.

As far as the generations who participated in the pre-Nazi elections are concerned—and they constitute the subject of our studies—it is fairly safe to predict that a majority, especially in the industrial and agricultural labor classes, will still be more or less in opposition to Hitler. Once the regime is defeated, it is very likely that even those rural and urban lower middle class groups from which came the main support of the Nazi party will revert to a political ideology more in agreement with their past political attitudes. The very lability of their party preferences in the pre-Nazi period should however caution us against any reliance on these forces.

The great enigma, the unknown quantity, is of course the younger generation of those who had not yet participated in political life when the National Socialists came to power and who therefore have had no experience with other forms of government. Too little is known about the present state of mind of this generation to justify any predictions.

However, one should not forget that these young men and women are the sons and daughters of former Conservatives, Liberals, Socialists, and so forth. In spite of all indoctrination and in spite of the undisputable restriction of family and home in their educational functions, it is quite unlikely that all transmission of sentiments, views, and opinions from the older to the younger generation through family and home relations should have ceased. In fact, one may assume that the younger generation, feeling firm in their status as Nazis, will more readily absorb whatever criticism of the regime they may encounter than the middle generation of Nazis who formed their opinions and beliefs during the years of struggle for power.

We should realize that the comparative ease with which the National Socialists actually seized power after Hitler had become Chancellor was largely due to the following circumstances: first, to the intimidating effect of strong local and regional successes in the elections of 1932. In this connection it is important to see that the federal structure of the Reich worked to the advantage of the Nazis. Their first experiments in government were made, not in Prussia, but in the smaller states of Brunswick, Thuringia, Oldenburg. That part of the latter which formed an enclave in Schleswig-Holstein served them as a strong-point whence they made their propaganda raids into the surrounding Prussian territory.

The overthrow of the old regime was facilitated, furthermore, by the fact that the Nazis had quietly penetrated practically every economic interest organization (with the exception of the labor unions) and every branch of the administrative and educational services; they were able to use these connections to obtain controlling positions in such organizations—this maneuver was part of their general tactics of intimidation. This they did like everything else in a piece-meal fashion, carefully avoiding such drastic steps as would have antagonized very large masses of the people at one time to such an extent as to make them willing to fight. Instead of prohibiting all opposition parties at once, they singled out the Communists, a measure by which they gained sympathy not only among the middle classes but even among the Social Democrats. Having dissolved the KPD, they did not immediately abolish the trade unions but waited until they had evidence that these would not fight back; this being accomplished, they proceeded to dissolve the SPD. The very gradual absorption of the Steel Helmets into the SA may be used as a further illustration; the gradually increased severity of anti-Semitic measures as another.

An additional factor which aided the Nazis in their entrenchment was that the opposition did not receive any direct or indirect support from the democracies. There were times during the first years of Hitler's regime when firm and determined measures to "stop" Hitler would have found enthusiastic mass support in Germany.

Only those who have had the experience of living under a charismatic tyranny, supported by a well-organized state and party bureaucracy, will really understand how gradually any oppositional action came to seem impossible or at least meaningless; how in an atmosphere of intimidation, hopeless resignation, and self-deceiving compromise, the masses succumbed to the rule of the militant and fanatical minority.

A great number of ingenious devices of "social control," aimed primarily at the attainment of conformity in overt behavior—the Hitler salute, the distribution of emblems in street collections, the pressing of people into the Nazi organizations—were developed with the result that it became increasingly difficult to abstain from more or less active support of the regime, while at the same time the danger of betraying one's heretic sentiments or ideas to an agent of the party became greater from month to month. Those who were discovered and fell into the hands of the authorities were, by Gestapo methods and secret trials, deprived even of the glory of martyrdom.

It is therefore not surprising that so little is known about the activities of anti-Nazi groups. One might rather say that it is astounding that under these conditions there have been any open oppositional activities at all. About these activities there is scanty but reliable direct information; that they are not insignificant can be inferred from repressive legislation and police measures and from the frantic threats of Nazi leaders; but there is no more cogent proof of the existence of an active opposition than the numerous executions of persons whose political stand is well known to many refugees from Nazi Germany. From the ranks of these active opposition groups will come the builders of a new democratic Germany.

SELECTED BIBLIOGRAPHY ON SCHLESWIG-HOLSTEIN

In Systematic Order

A. General

Brandt, O. *Geschichte Schleswig-Holsteins, ein Grundriss,* Kiel, 1925.

Von Hedemann-Heespen, P. *Schleswig-Holstein und die Neuzeit,* Kiel, 1926.

Sering, M. *Die Deutsche Landwirtschaft unter Volks—und Weltwirtschaftlichen Gesichtspunkten,* Berlin, 1932.

Sering, M., Niehaus, H., and Schloemer, F. *Deutsche Agrarpolitik auf Geschichtlicher und Landeskundlicher Grundlage* (Prepared for the International Conference of Agricultural Economists), Leipzig, 1934.

Wuebbena. *Ueber die Arbeitsverhaeltnisse in der Provinz Schleswig-Holstein, Arbeiten der Landwirtschaftskammer,* No. 2, Kiel, 1900.

Fallada, Hans (pseudonym). *Bauern, Bomben und Bonzen.*

Von Salomon, E. *Die Stadt.*

Bielfeldt. *Ueber Kapitalumlauf in Landwirtschaftlichen Betrieben Schleswig-Holsteins* (Unpublished Dissertation), Kiel, ca. 1934.

Danker, E. *Die Verschuldung der Schleswig-Holsteinischen Landwirtschaft in Ihrer Regionalen Bedingtheit,* Kiel, 1931.

Peters, Ch. *Die Entwicklung der Landwirtschaftlichen Kreditorganisation in der Provinz Schleswig-Holstein in der Nachkriegszeit* (Dissertation), Kiel, 1931.

Traulsen, H. *Wirtschaftserfolg und Intensitaetsgrenzen Baeuerlicher Veredelungswirtschaft in Schleswig-Holstein,* Kiel, 1931.

B. Subregions

Cornils, P. W. *Die Communalverfassung in Eiderstedt,* Heide, 1841.

Pauls, V. *Landesherrschaft und Selbstverwaltung in Eiderstedt*, Garding, 1932.

Frenssen, Gustav. *Joern Uhl*, Berlin, 1901.

Feddersen, J. *Die Rindviehweidemast in Schleswig-Holstein*, Schwerin i. M., 1921.

Langenheim, K. *Das Absatzproblem in der Fettweidewirtschaft der Schleswig-Holsteinischen Marschen*, 1936.

Wode, H. *Rentabilitaetsfragen der Marschwirtschaften in Schleswig-Holstein* (Dissertation), Kiel, 1932.

Dethlefsen. *Geschichte der Holsteinischen Elbmarschen*, Glueckstadt, 1892.

Heimatbuch des Kreises Pinneberg, 1928.

Lange, H. H. *Die Gewerbliche Schweinemast in den Kreisen York, Sueder-Dithmarschen, Steinburg, Pinneberg und Syke* (Dissertation), Halle-Wittenberg, 1928.

Nagel, I. "Beitrag zur Siedlungskunde und Bevoelkerungsverteilung des Kreises Steinburg," *Heimatbuch des Kreises Steinburg*, ca. 1928.

Hermberg, P. *Die Bevoelkerung des Kirchspiels Muensterdorf* (Dissertation), Kiel, 1913.

Kroeger, K. *Untersuchungen ueber die Landwirtschaftlichen Betriebsverhaeltnisse auf der Geest in Schleswig-Holstein*, Kiel, 1931.

Doose, R. *Die Entwicklung der Wirtschaftlichen Verhaeltnisse in der Probstei, Arbeiten der Landwirtschaftskammer fuer die Provinz Schleswig-Holstein*, No. 14, Kiel, 1910.

Hanssen, Georg. *Historisch-Statistische Darstellung der Insel Fehmarn*, Altona, 1832.

Von Hedemann-Heespen, P. *Geschichte des Gutes Deutsch-Nienhof*.

Jessen, Jens. "Die Entstehung und Entwicklung der Gutswirtschaft in Schleswig-Holstein," *Zeitschrift fuer Schleswig-Holsteinische Geschichte 51*, Band Kiel, 1922.

Staehly, A. *Untersuchung ueber die Entwicklung des Landwirtschaftlichen Bodenbesitzes und der Betriebsverhaeltnisse Ostholsteins unter Besonderer Beruecksichtigung der Zeitpachtdoerfer* (Dissertation), Berlin, 1929.

Jensen, H. N. A. *Angeln, Geschichtlich und Topographisch,* 1844.
Neu Bearbeitet und bis auf die Gegenwart Fortgefuehrt von W.
Martensen und J. Henningsen, Schleswig, 1922.

Pfeiffer, G. *Das Siedlungsbild der Landschaft Angeln, Schriften
der Baltischen Kommission zu Kiel,* No. 14, Breslau, 1928.